16 EASY FOR FING

S R

Quick & Easy Fingerstyle Guitar Arrangements

By Troy Nelson

ISBN 9798686570580   Copyright © 2020 Troy Nelson Music LLC
International Copyright Secured. All Rights Reserved.

HOW TO GET THE AUDIO

The audio files for this book are available for free as downloads or streaming on *troynelsonmusic.com*.

We are available to help you with your audio downloads and any other questions you may have. Simply email *help@troynelsonmusic.com*.

See below for the recommended ways to listen to the audio:

Download Audio Files (Zipped)	Stream Audio Files
• Download Audio Files (Zipped)	• Recommended for CELL PHONES & TABLETS
• Recommended for COMPUTERS on WiFi	• Bookmark this page
• A ZIP file will automatically download to the default "downloads" folder on your computer	• Simply tap the PLAY button on the track you want to listen to
• Recommended: download to a desktop/laptop computer *first*, then transfer to a tablet or cell phone	• Files also available for streaming or download at *soundcloud.com/troynelsonbooks*
• Phones & tablets may need an "unzipping" app such as iZip, Unrar or Winzip	
• Download on WiFi for faster download speeds	

To download the companion audio files for this book, visit: troynelsonmusic.com/audio-downloads/

INTRODUCTION

Nothing brings out the emotion of a song quite like fingerpicking. The warm tone generated by bare fingers on the guitar strings is an intoxicating sound that some guitarists spend their whole lives chasing.

Fingerpicking can take songs in a direction not afforded by traditional flatpicking, namely because the former enables the guitarist to pluck multiple—and specific—strings simultaneously to create beautiful, lush chord-melody arrangements that are unattainable with only a pick. To hear the difference firsthand, listen to the audio examples that accompany this book. The melody-only tracks are performed with a medium-gauge nylon pick and sound bright and punchy. Meanwhile, the chord-melody tracks are performed with bare fingers and sound warm and inviting—the prefect tone for the holiday season!

If fingerpicking, or fingerstyle, guitar is new to you, the concept is fairly simple (although the technique itself will take some time to master). Generally, the thumb handles the notes on the bass strings (low E, A, and D), while the remaining fingers—index, middle, and ring—are assigned to the treble strings (G, B, and high E).

This is not a hard-and-fast rule, by any means. In fact, deciding which fingers will handle which strings is typically decided by the chord voicing and the strings that need to be plucked. Because of this, we've included pick-hand fingerings for all 16 songs: *p* = thumb, *i* = index, *m* = middle, and *a* = ring.

Use these fingerings, which are notated below the chord-melody tab staff, as a guide as you learn the songs. If any of them feel awkward, feel free to experiment with fingerings of your own, as the ones notated in the book are merely suggestions. That said, you shouldn't deviate too far from the basic principles of fingerstyle guitar that were stated earlier: using the thumb for the bass strings and the other three fingers for the treble strings.

Each song in this book contains four components: lyrics, melody, chords, and a fingerpicked chord melody. If you're unfamiliar with the latter, *chord melody* is simply an arrangement that includes both the melody and the harmony (chords), enabling a guitarist to play solo or in a setting that lacks another melodic/harmonic instrument, such as a drum/bass/guitar trio. More specifically, the melody and chords are played *at the same time*. The chords are generally plucked as they occur in the arrangement and in a fairly consistent rhythm—for example, on beats 1 and 3 of each measure (in 4/4 time)—while the melody is played on top. This means that chords are often altered a bit in order to play the melody note on the top string of the chord voicing.

Although fingerstyle chord melody is the central component, you'll have other options for performing the songs in this book, as well. For example, if you're performing with another guitarist or piano player, you could play the melody (notated in the top tab staff, above the chord melody) while he/she handles chord duty.

Chord frames are also included wherever they occur so, if you're a vocalist, you could strum and sing Christmas songs to your friends and relatives. Just follow the suggested strum patterns that are presented in the introductions to the songs and listen to the audio examples to help you get started. One thing you'll notice as you play through the songs is how the top notes of the chord melody mirror the notes of the song's melody, and how the chords in the chord melody are derived from the voicings in the chord frames above the staff.

Chord melody is synonymous with jazz, but in lieu of the more sophisticated extended and altered chords of that genre, the arrangements in this book are limited to common open chords. In fact, the majority of songs contain just 3–5 chords.

While absolute beginners may struggle a bit with some of these arrangements, late beginners and intermediate players should be able to pick them up fairly quickly. And sight-reading these songs is certainly not out of the question for advanced guitarists.

READING CHORD DIAGRAMS & TAB

As mentioned in the introduction, the songs in this book are presented in both chord diagrams and in tab. In this section, we're going to go over each format so you'll be able to quickly apply the music to your instrument. Let's start with chord diagrams.

Chord Diagrams

A *chord diagram*, or *chord frame*, is simply a graphical representation of a small section (usually four or five frets) of the guitar neck, or fretboard. Vertical lines represent the guitar's six strings, horizontal lines represent frets, and black dots indicate where your fingers should be placed. Although a bit counterintuitive, chord diagrams are presented as though you're looking at the neck while the guitar is held vertically in front of you, rather than from a more natural horizontal position. Nevertheless, chord frames are a good way to quickly understand how a chord should be "voiced," or fingered.

A thick, black horizontal line at the top of the diagram indicates the guitar's nut (the plastic-like string-spacer at the end of the fretboard). When this is present, the chord typically incorporates one or more open strings, which are represented by hollow circles above the frame. Conversely, when an open string is not to be played, an "X" will appear above the frame.

When more than one note is fretted by the same finger, or "barred," a slur encompasses those notes, which can range from two to six strings (*barre chords* get their name from this technique). If a chord is played higher up the neck, above the 4th or 5th fret, the nut is replaced by a thin horizontal line and the fret number is indicated next to the lowest fret (highest in the diagram). Sometimes—but not always—the chord's fingering is included at the bottom of the frame: 1 = index, 2 = middle, 3 = ring, 4 = pinky, and T = thumb.

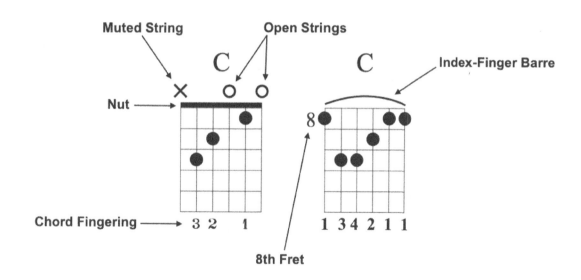

Tab

As a form of music notation, tab has been around for centuries. However, it has really exploded in popularity among guitar players the past few decades, particularly since the advent of the Internet. The reason for its popularity is the simple fact that it's so easy to learn and use.

A tab staff looks much like a standard music staff; however, if you look a little closer, you'll notice that it contains *six* lines instead of five. Those six lines represent the six strings of the guitar, with the low E string positioned at the bottom, and the high E string at the top. Tab contains no key signature because note-reading is not involved; instead, numbers are placed on the strings to represent the frets of the guitar neck. For example, if you see the number 3 on the low E (6th) string, you would press down on fret 3 of that string. Or, if you see the number 0 stacked on the D and G (4th and 3rd) strings, you would pluck those two strings together, open (unfretted).

Sometimes, you'll see tab accompanied by standard notation, and other times, you'll see tab-only music. Like standard notation, tab-only music often includes rhythms (stems, flags, beams, rests, etc.). Rhythm symbols in tab are the same as the ones you'll find in standard notation, only the noteheads are replaced by fret numbers.

Regardless of what type of tab is used, a time signature will be present. The *time signature* is a pair of numbers stacked on top of each other at the beginning of a piece of music (immediately after the key signature in standard notation). The top number indicates how many beats comprise each *measure*, or *bar* (the space between the vertical *bar lines*), while the bottom number indicates which note is equivalent to one beat (2 = half note, 4 = quarter note, 8 = eighth note, etc.). Ten of the songs in this book are played in 4/4 time, meaning each measure contains four beats (upper number) and quarter notes are equivalent to one beat (bottom number), while the other six songs are played in 3/4 time, and each measure contains three beats.

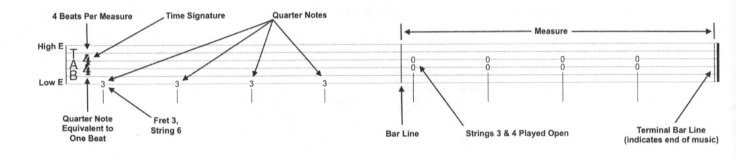

THE CHORDS

As mentioned in the introduction, the chord voicings for each song are illustrated above the staffs, but let's preview the chords here in case some of them are new to you.

The 13 chords below serve two purposes: 1) they're the voicings you'll strum if you plan to strum and sing the songs, and 2) they provide the framework for the chords used in the fingerstyle chord-melody arrangements. If you're unfamiliar with any of these chords, get to know them now. That way, you'll be ready to jump in and learn any one of the 16 songs.

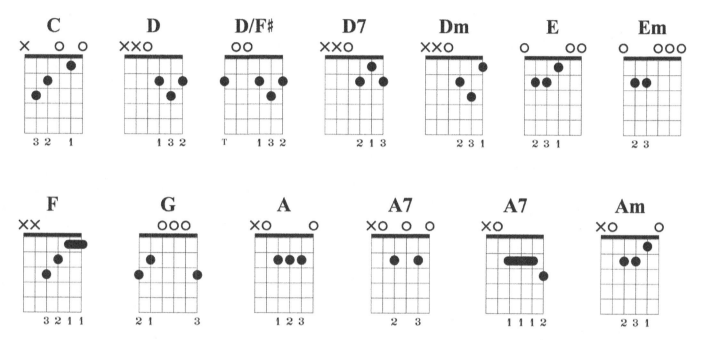

As you start to learn the chord melodies, you'll quickly discover that alternative chord voicings and fingerings must be employed. Below are 10 voicings that are either entirely new chord types (Cadd9, Fadd9, F6, Gmaj7, G7, Esus4, and Asus4) or are alternate fingerings for some of the chords on the previous page (C and G). Despite these new chord types/fingerings, the 13 chords on the previous page are still the fundamental chords of the arrangements. Get to know these alternate chords, as well, as they will come in handy very soon.

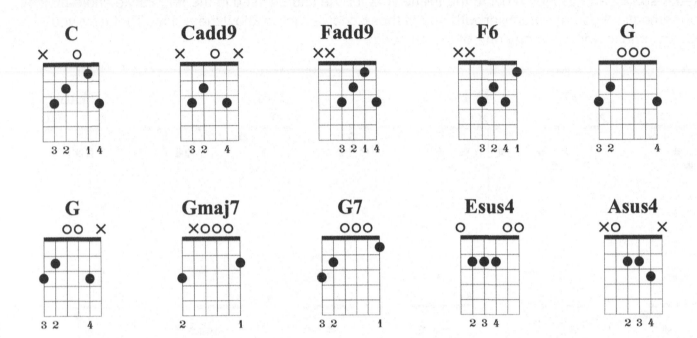

HOW TO CHANGE KEYS

All 16 songs in this book are arranged in one of three keys—C, G, or Am. However, if you prefer to play any of them in a different key, all you need is a capo. If you're unfamiliar, a *capo* is a device that clamps onto the guitar's neck to shorten the length of the strings, thereby transposing the music to another key, which is determined by the fret on which the capo is placed.

The following diagrams will help with changing keys. The first diagram illustrates the various keys on the neck when using the open C chord as the tonic chord. For example, to play in the key of C♯, simply place the capo on fret 1 and strum the C chord (index finger should now be on fret 2). To play in the key of D, just slide the capo up to fret 2 (and voice the C chord at fret 3).

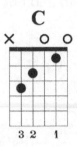

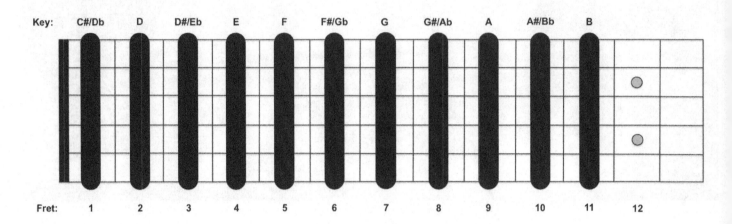

The same principle applies to the open G chord. For example, to play in the key of A, place the capo at fret 2 and strum the G chord (now voiced with the middle finger on fret 5 of string 6). To play in the key of B, simply slide the capo up to fret 4 and strum the G chord (now voiced on fret 7).

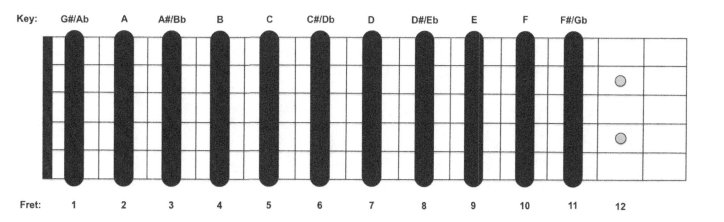

We can use a capo to change minor keys, as well. For example, to play in the key of Bm, place the capo at fret 2 and strum the Am chord (now voiced with the index finger on fret 3, string 2). To play in the key of Dm, simply slide the capo up to fret 5 and strum the Am chord (now voiced on fret 6).

Am

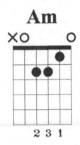

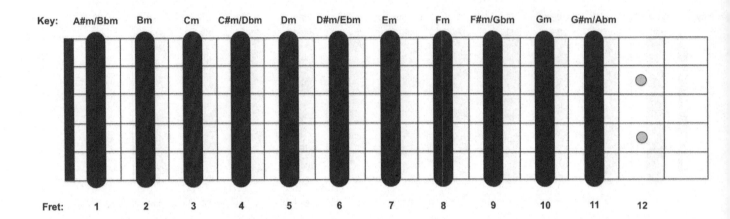

When using a capo while playing the chord melodies, it's important to remember that the tab numbers are relative to the capoed fret. In other words, the capoed fret acts as the nut, so when you see a "0" (zero) in tab, you should still play the string "open," but now it rings at a higher pitch due to the capo's position on the neck.

The other tab numbers are relative to the capo, as well, so when you see a "1" on, say, the low E string, you should voice that string on the fret directly adjacent to the capo. For example, if the capo is placed on fret 5, you would voice that note on fret 6, which is fret 1 ("1") in tab. In other words, just envision the capoed fret as the open strings ("0" in tab) and play all other notes accordingly.

14

ANGELS WE HAVE HEARD ON HIGH

KEY: C

CHORDS: C, G, and F

TIP: You'll want to use the alternate voicing for the G chord so you can quickly and efficiently switch between C and G chords, playing the melody notes on strings 1–2 with the pinky. The G7 voicing will come into play a few times, as well, so be sure go back to the introduction and review these chords before diving into the song.

WATCH OUT FOR: The chorus. The single notes played along strings 1 and 2 in bars 1–3 and 7–9 are tricky to perform—and especially tricky to perform in time—so be sure to listen to the audio examples to hear how they should be phrased. The tendency is to rush the slides and pull-offs, but they should be played as straight, even 8th notes.

STRUM PATTERN:

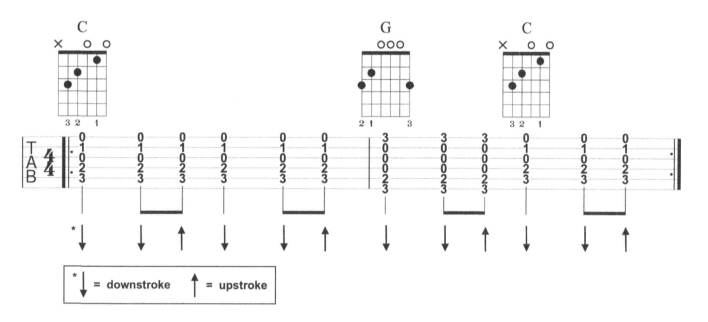

Angels We Have Heard on High

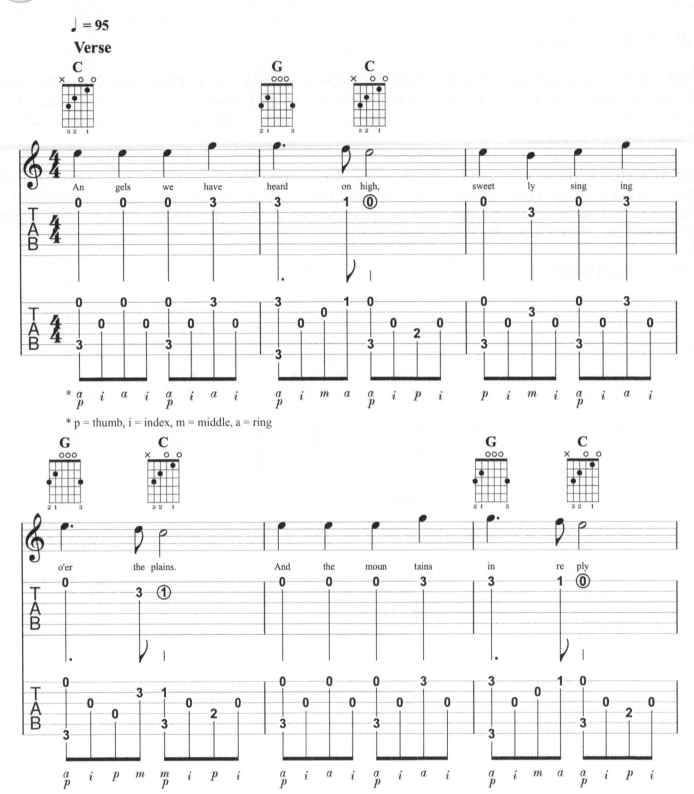

* p = thumb, i = index, m = middle, a = ring

16

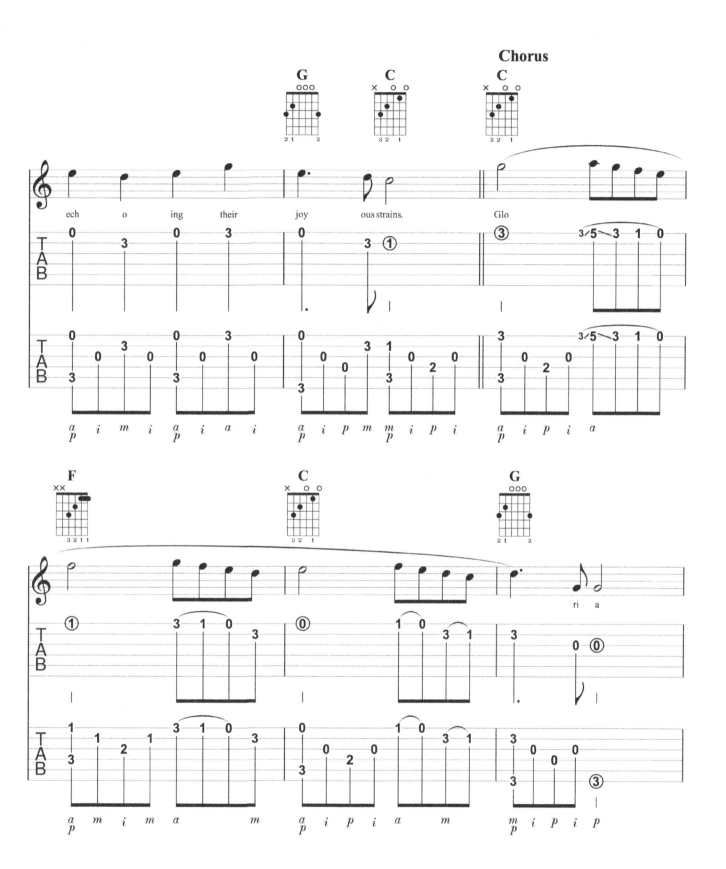

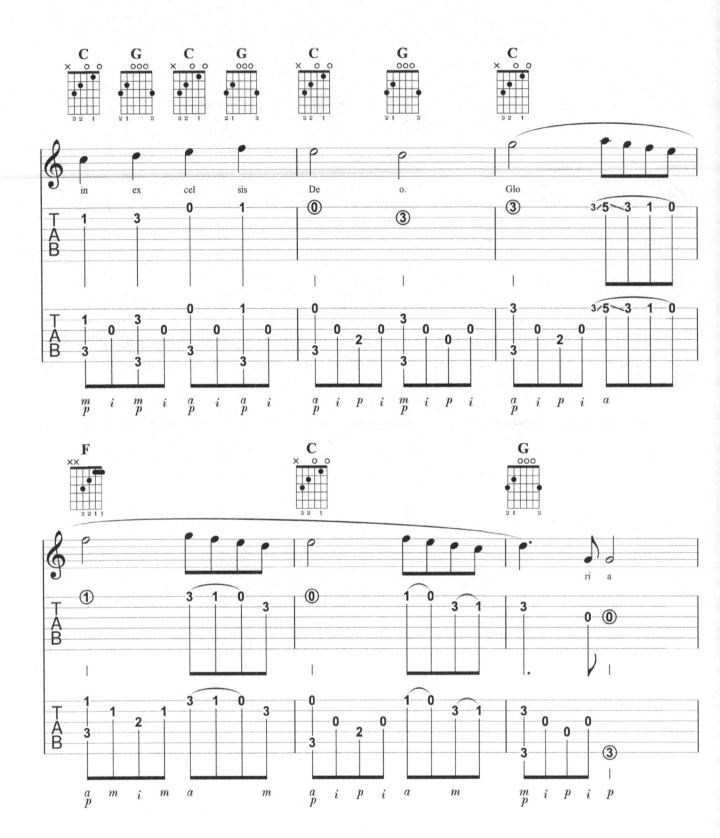

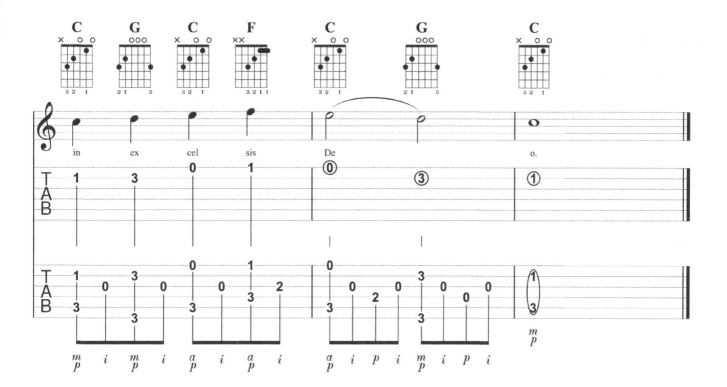

Additional Lyrics

2. Shepherds, why this jubilee?
   Why your joyous strains prolong?
   What the gladsome tidings be
   Which inspire your heavenly song?
   Gloria in excelsis Deo
   Gloria in excelsis Deo

3. Come to Bethlehem and see
   Him whose birth the angels sing
   Come adore on bended knee
   Christ the Lord, the newborn King
   Gloria in excelsis Deo
   Gloria in excelsis Deo

AULD LANG SYNE

KEY: G

CHORDS: G, D/F♯, C, and Em

TIP: Although the D/F♯ chord frame suggests voicing the F♯ note on string 6 with your thumb, the most efficient way to perform the chord melody is to shift the middle finger from fret 3 to fret 2 on string 6 when moving from G to D/F♯, and then adding the ring finger to fret 2 of string 3 for the A melody note.

WATCH OUT FOR: The F♯ melody note (fret 4, string 4) in bar 1. The best way to grab this note is to voice the G chord normally (i.e., as suggested in the chord frame) and use your pinky to voice the pitch. Because of the awkward stretch, the biggest challenge here is voicing the note accurately. But don't get discouraged; it'll come with a little practice.

STRUM PATTERN:

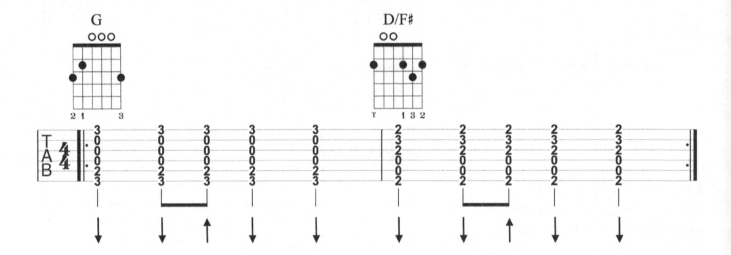

Auld Lang Syne

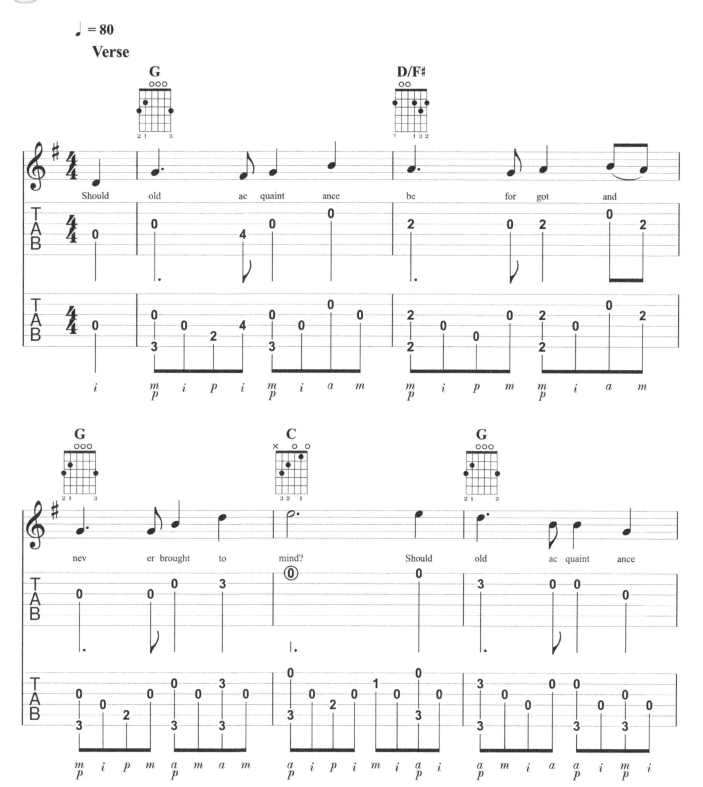

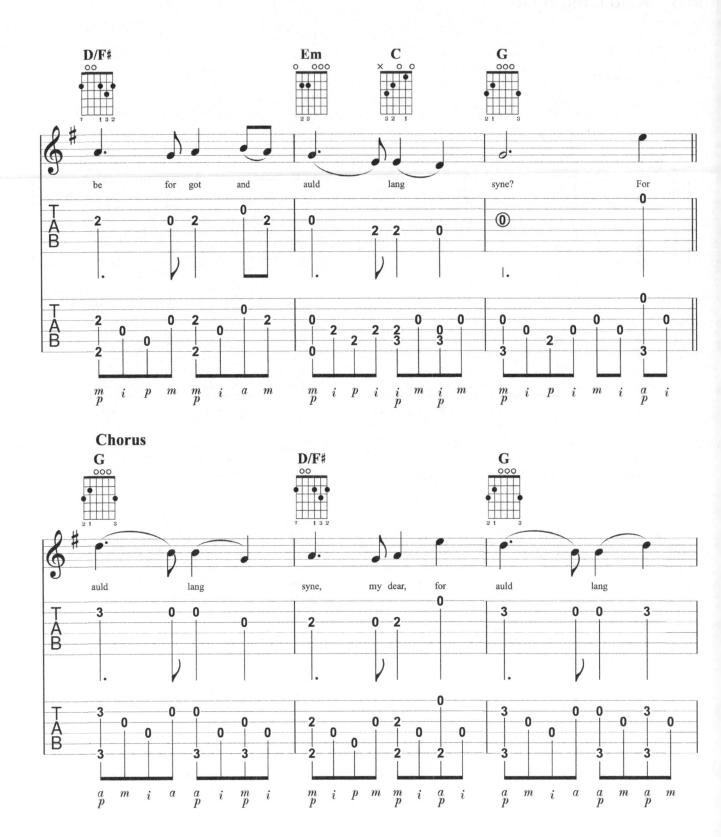

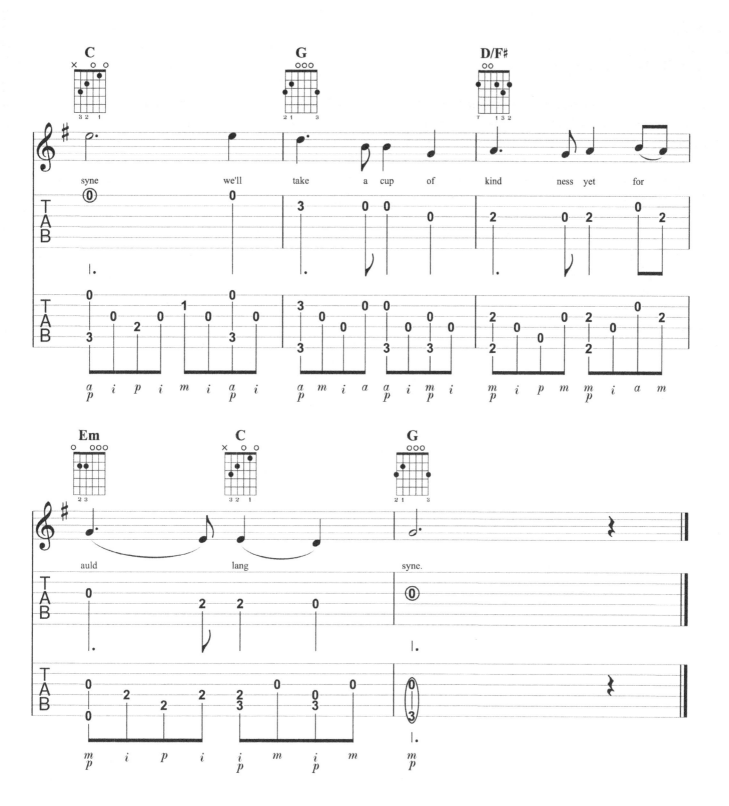

AWAY IN A MANGER

KEY: C

CHORDS: C, F, and G

TIP: When playing fingerstyle arrangements like these, one of the goals is to allow chord tones to ring out as long as possible while playing the melody on top. Therefore, whenever possible, keep the chord shapes voiced while you play the melody notes. For example, in bars 1–2, keep your ring finger affixed to fret 3 of string 5 as you voice the melody notes on strings 1–2 with your index and pinky fingers. Similarly, in bar 3, keep your ring and middle fingers in place for the F chord while you remove your index finger from fret 1 to play the second melody note of the measure, B (your middle finger should already be in place for the A melody note on fret 2 of string 3).

WATCH OUT FOR: Measure 13. Here, the melody jumps up to a high F note over a G chord. This creates a wide ring-index finger stretch that should be handle with the G7 voicing presented in the book's introduction.

STRUM PATTERN:

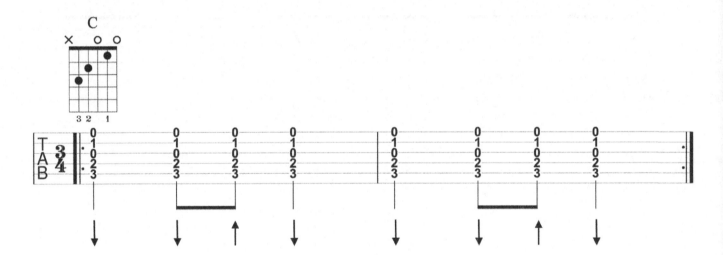

Away in a Manger

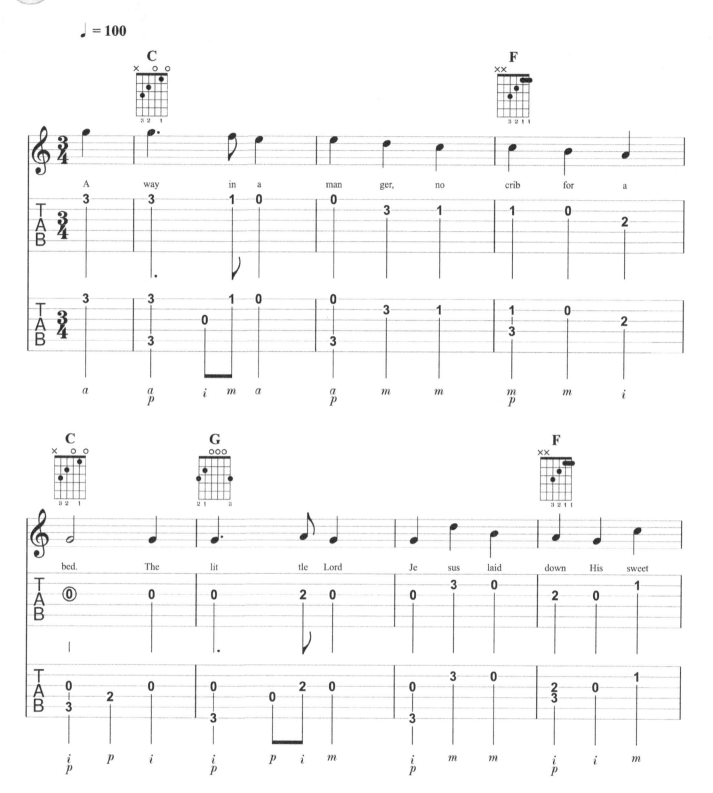

Additional Lyrics

2. The Cattle are lowing, the baby awakes
   But little Lord Jesus no crying he makes
   I love Thee, Lord Jesus; look down from the sky
   And stay by my cradle 'til morning is nigh

3. Be near me, Lord Jesus; I ask Thee to stay
   Close by me forever and love me, I pray
   Bless all the dear children in thy tender care
   And take us to heaven, to live with Thee there

DECK THE HALLS

KEY: G

CHORDS: G, Am, D, A7, Em, and C

TIP: For the quick D–A7–D chord change in bar 12, start with the open D chord voicing shown in the chord frame above the staff and keep it in place throughout the measure. In other words, since the A7 change consists of plucking two open strings (A and high E), there's no need to change your fingering. Just be sure to adjust which strings you target when you return to the D chord on beat 3 (i.e., pluck strings 2 and 4 instead of strings 1 and 4).

WATCH OUT FOR: Bars 4 and 8. In those two measures, grabbing the F♯ note (fret 4, string 4) while quickly switching from (and to) the G chord is challenging. The best approach is to use your pinky to voice the note while plucking the strings with a thumb-index combination. If you struggle with this double-stop, you can omit the open A string, which is simply included to add some heft to the chord, and just pluck the fretted note (F♯).

STRUM PATTERN:

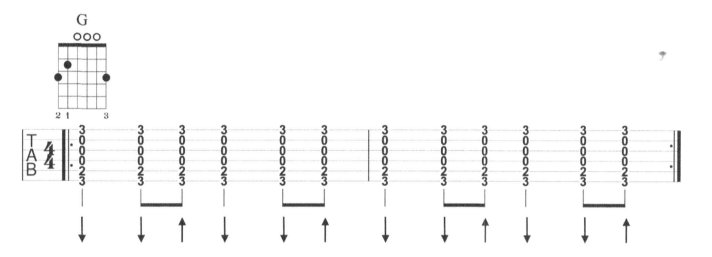

Deck the Halls

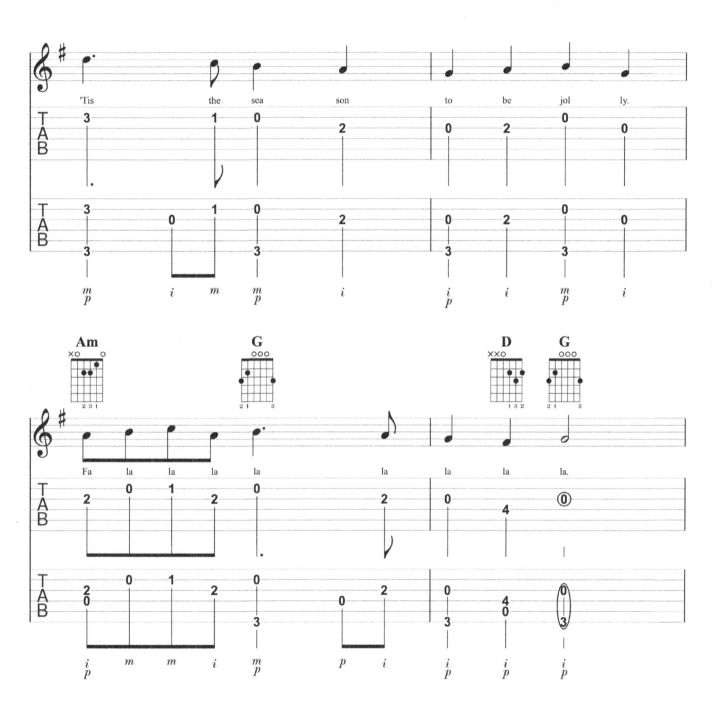

'Tis the sea son to be jol ly.

Fa la la la la la la la la.

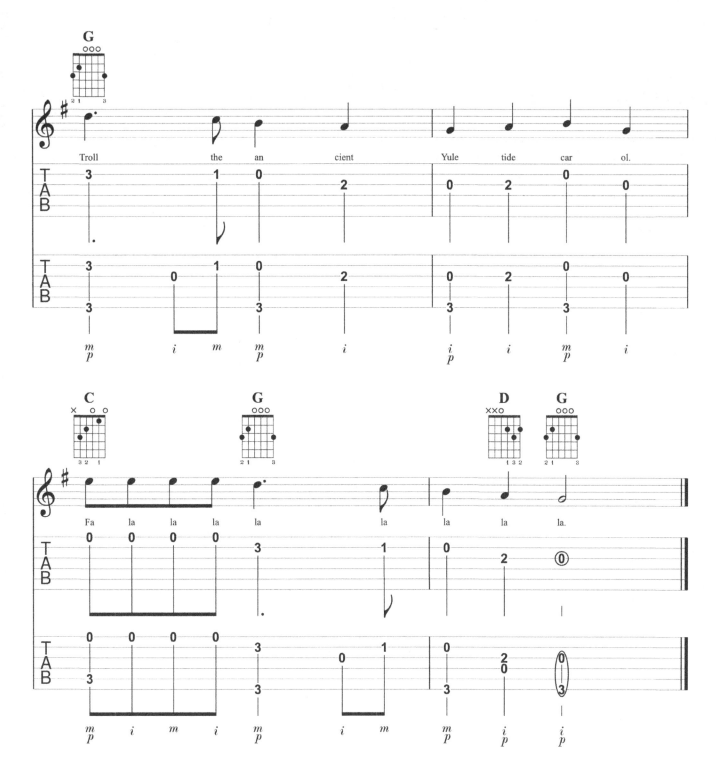

Additional Lyrics

2. See the blazing yule before us
   Fa, la, la, la, la, la, la, la, la
   Strike the harp and join the chorus
   Fa, la, la, la, la, la, la, la, la
   Follow me in merry measure
   Fa, la, la, la, la, la, la, la, la
   While I tell of yuletide treasure
   Fa, la, la, la, la, la, la, la, la

3. Fast away the old year passes
   Fa, la, la, la, la, la, la, la, la
   Hail the new, ye lads and lasses
   Fa, la, la, la, la, la, la, la, la
   Sing we joyous all together
   Fa, la, la, la, la, la, la, la, la
   Heedless of the wind and weather
   Fa, la, la, la, la, la, la, la, la

31

THE FIRST NOEL

KEY: G

CHORDS: G, D, C, and Em

TIP: Start the song with your fret-hand fingers voicing the alternate version of the G chord (shown in the introduction). That way, your fingers are already in place for the opening chord of the song. As for the pickup notes, voice the A note (fret 2, string 3) with the middle finger of your fret hand (your ring finger should be in place at fret 3 of string 6).

WATCH OUT FOR: Bars 7 and 15. In these two measures, you'll use the alternate version of the C chord so you can voice the high G melody note (fret 3, string 1) with your pinky. But the real challenge here is quickly shifting the pinky from string 1 to string 2 on consecutive beats—and on the same fret. It's an awkward move at first, so practice this measure in isolation several times before tackling the whole song.

STRUM PATTERN:

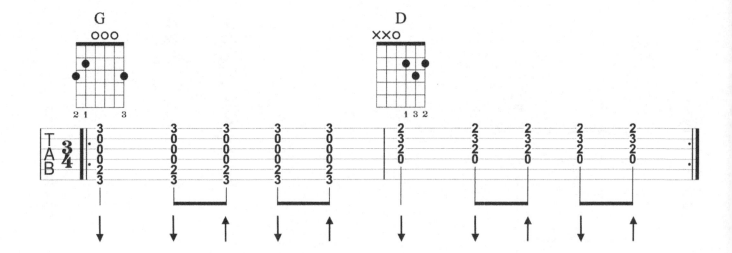

The First Noel

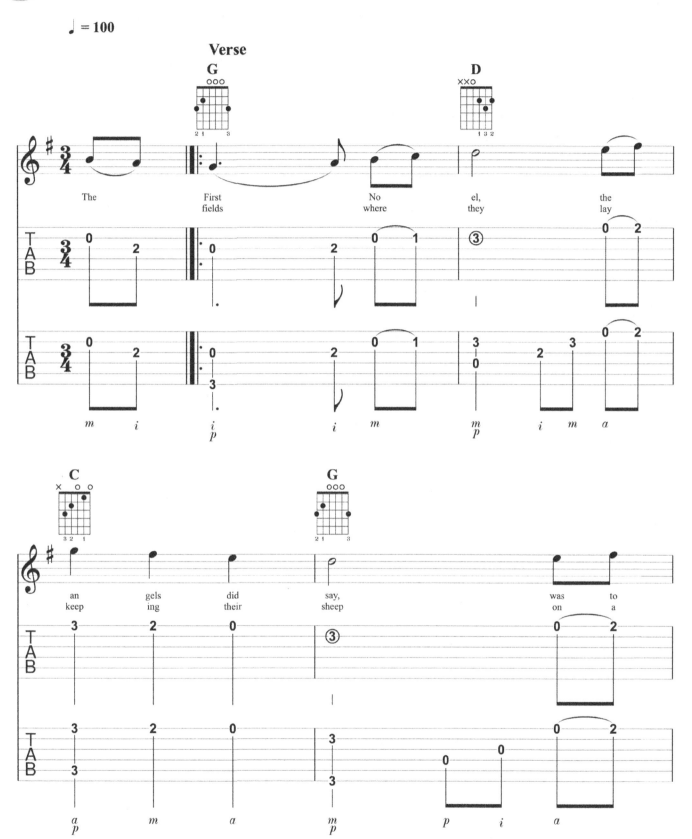

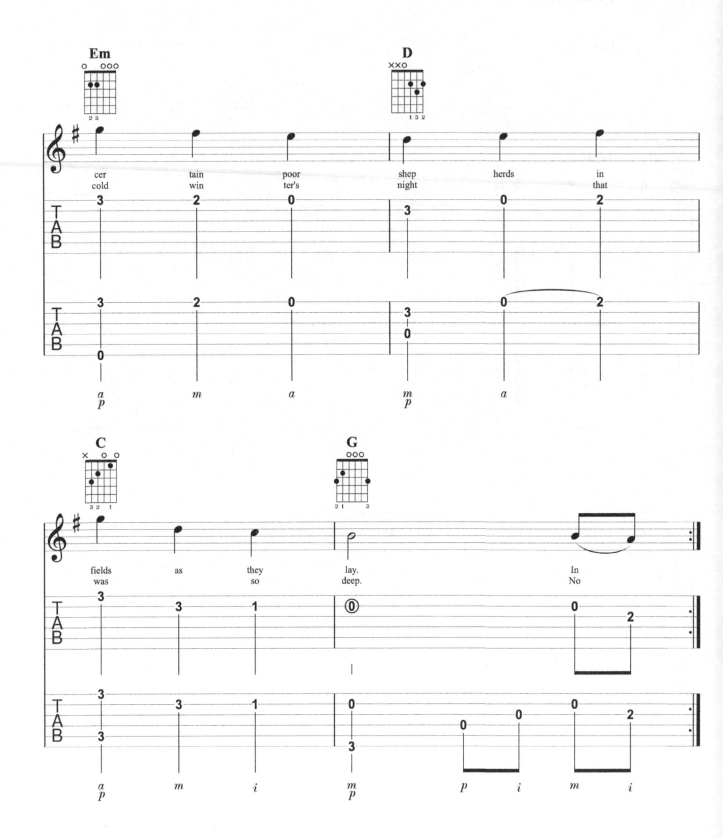

Chorus

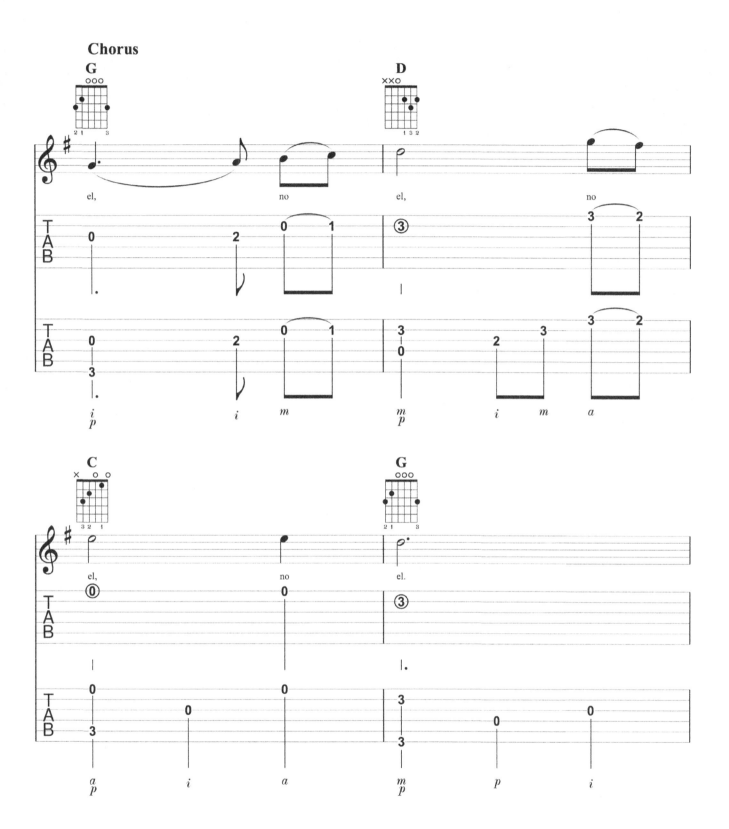

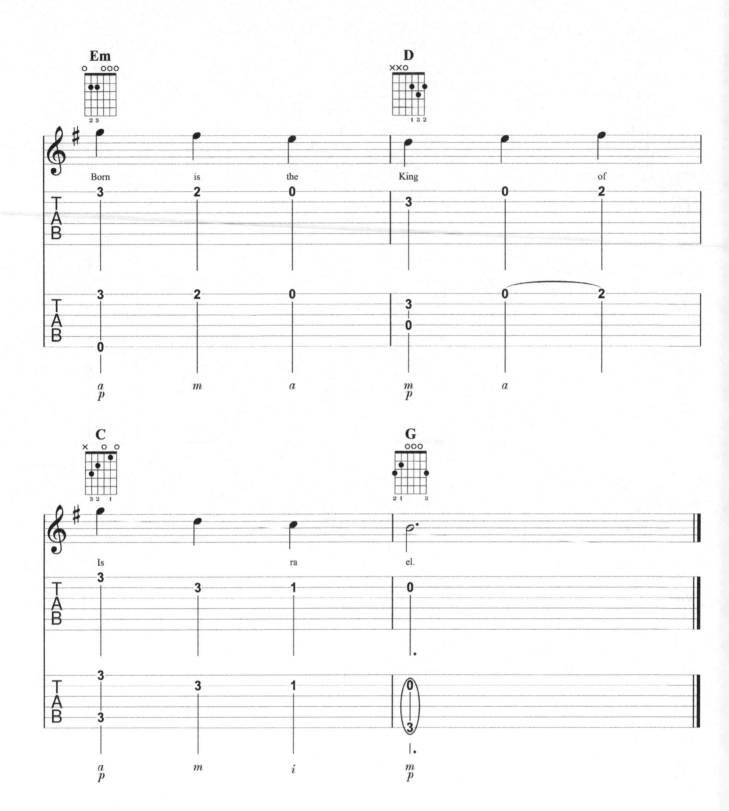

2. They looked up and saw a star
   Shining in the East beyond them far
   And to the earth it gave great light
   And so it continued both day and night
   Noel, Noel, Noel, Noel
   Born is the King of Israel

3. And by the light of the same star
   Three wisemen came from country far
   To seek for a King was their intent
   And to follow the star wherever it went
   Noel, Noel, Noel, Noel
   Born is the King of Israel

4. This star drew nigh to the Northwest
   O'er Bethlehem it took its rest
   And there it did both pause and stay
   Right o'er the place where Jesus lay
   Noel, Noel, Noel, Noel
   Born is the King of Israel

5. Then entered in those wisemen three
   Full reverently upon their knee
   And offered there in His Presence
   Their gold and myrrh and frankincense
   Noel, Noel, Noel, Noel
   Born is the King of Israel

6. Then let us all with one accord
   Sing praise to our heavenly Lord
   That hath made Heaven and earth of nought
   And with his blood mankind hath bought
   Noel, Noel, Noel, Noel
   Born is the King of Israel

GO TELL IT ON THE MOUNTAIN

KEY: G

CHORDS: G, D, Am, A, and D7

TIP: Use the more traditional version of the open G chord—the one shown in the chord frame above the staff—throughout this song. That way, you can use your index finger to voice all of the fretted melody notes on fret 2 (strings 3–5).

WATCH OUT FOR: Measures 1 and 5. The 8th-note run on beats 3–4 is easy to rush, so be sure to use a metronome to keep time while practicing the song. And, as always, listen to the audio demonstration to hear how the passage should sound. One thing you'll notice is that the 8th notes are swung; that is, the first 8th note of each 8th-note pair is held slightly longer than the second. This shuffle feel is illustrated at the top of the song, just below the tempo marking.

STRUM PATTERN:

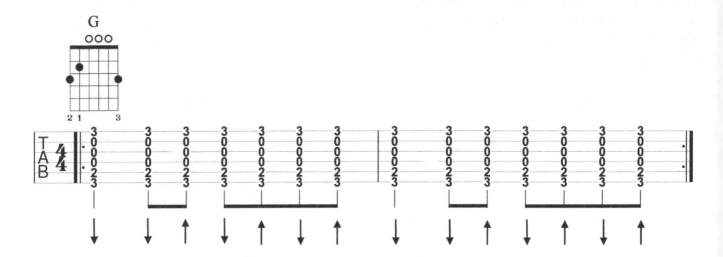

Go Tell It on the Mountain

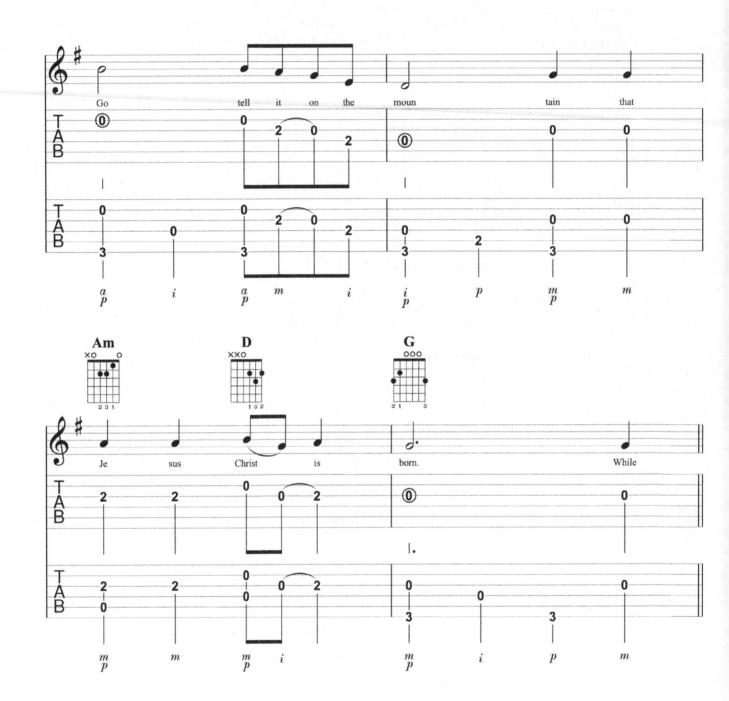

41

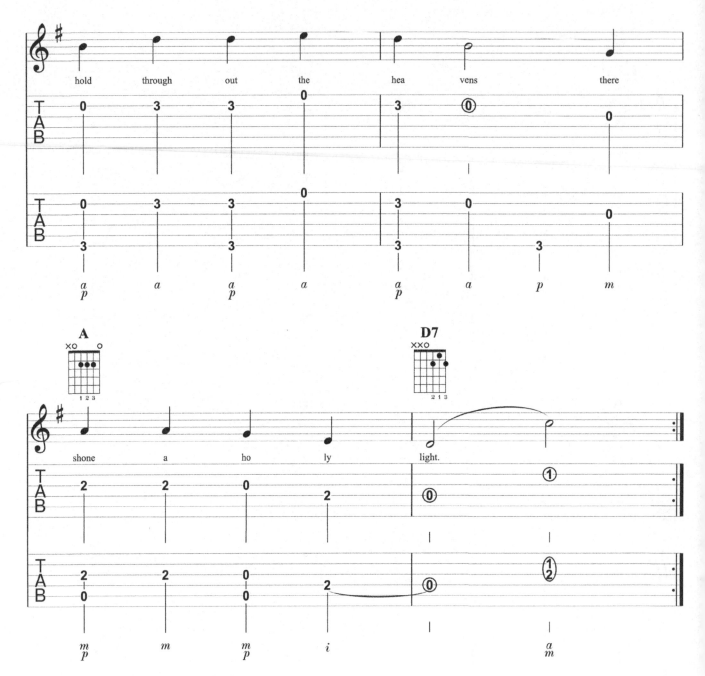

Additional Lyrics

2. The shepherds feared and trembled
   When lo above the earth
   Rang out the angel chorus
   That hailed our Savior's birth

3. Down in a lowly manger
   Our humble Christ was born
   And God sent us salvation
   That blessed Christmas morn

JINGLE BELLS

KEY: C

CHORDS: C, F, and G

TIP: In the chorus, when moving from the F chord (bar 5) to the C chord (bar 6), keep your index finger barred across strings 1–2 at fret 1 while you shift your ring finger from string 4 to string 5. This maneuver can be repeated in bars 13–14, as well.

WATCH OUT FOR: Measure 15 of the verse. Here, the melody jumps up to the high A note at fret 5 of string 1 while the harmony stays on the G chord from the preceding measure. The most efficient way to play this measure 15, as well as measure 14, is to barre your index finger across all six strings at fret 3 and use your ring finger to grab the A note on string 1 and your pinky to grab the F note at fret 6 of string 2 (your index finger will handle all notes on fret 3, of course).

STRUM PATTERN:

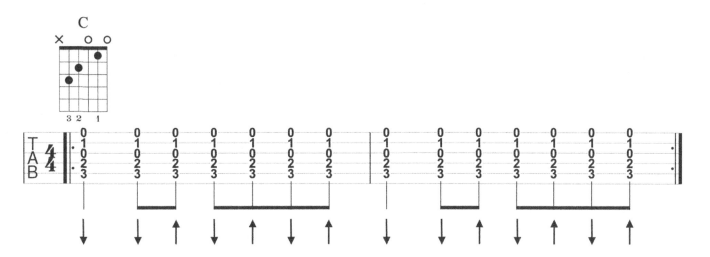

Jingle Bells

44

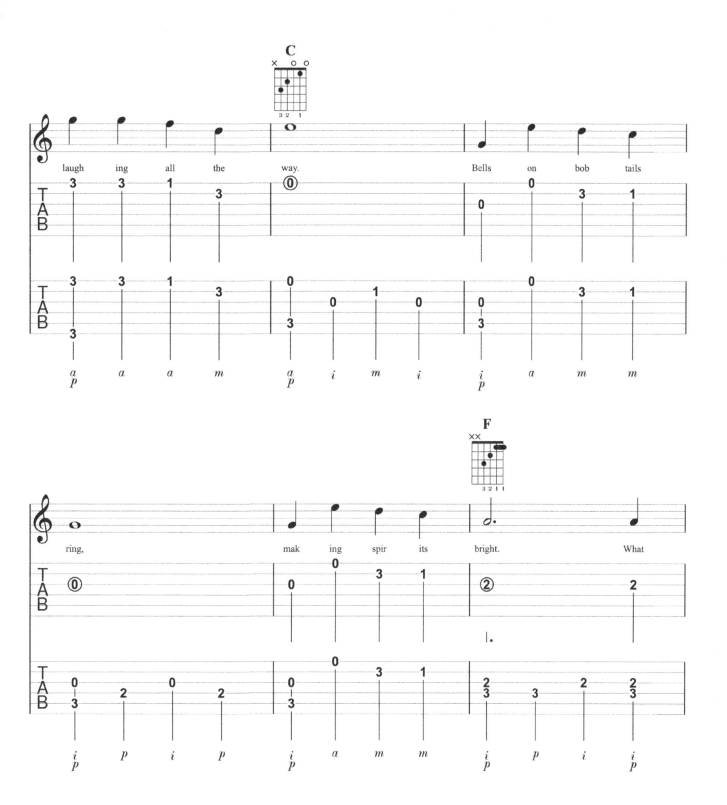

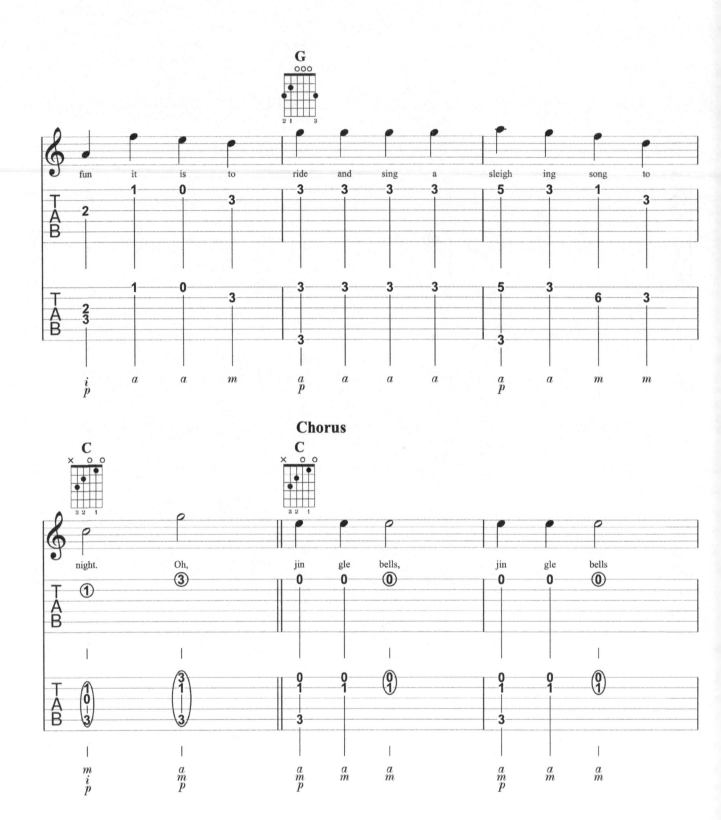

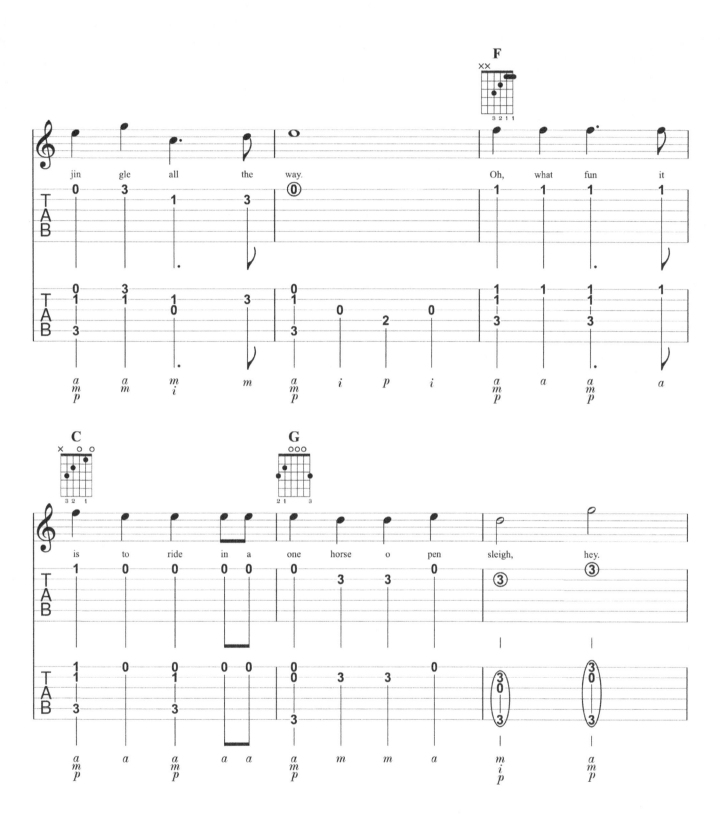

47

48

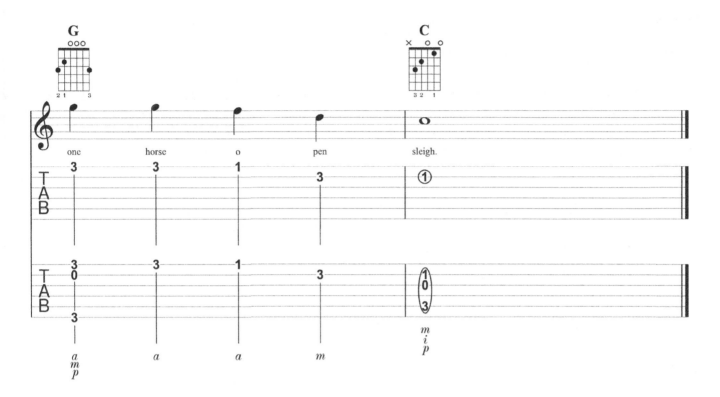

one   horse   o   pen   sleigh.

Additional Lyrics

2. A day or two ago
   I thought I'd take a ride
   And soon Miss Fanny Bright
   Was seated by my side
   The horse was lean and lank
   Misfortune seemed his lot
   He got into a drifted bank
   And then we got upsot

3. A day or two ago
   The story I must tell
   I went out on the snow
   And on my back I fell
   A gent was riding by
   In a one-horse open sleigh
   He laughed as there I sprawling lie
   But quickly drove away

4. Now the ground is white
   Go it while you're young
   Take the girls tonight
   And sing this sleighing song
   Just get a bobtailed bay
   Two forty as his speed
   Hitch him to an open sleigh
   And crack, you'll take the lead

JOY TO THE WORLD

KEY: G

CHORDS: G, Em, D/F♯, C, and D

TIP: Start this song with the G chord fingering suggested in the chord frame above the staff, quickly moving to the Gmaj7 voicing presented in the book's introduction on beat 3. At bar 2, shift your ring finger from string 1 to string 2 while keeping your middle finger in place at fret 3 of string 6. When you get to beat 4, simply grab the C melody note (fret 1, string 2) with you index finger (you can release your middle and ring fingers, as well, since open strings are played at the top of bar 3).

WATCH OUT FOR: Measures 13 and 15. Rhythmically, these two measures pick up the pace via a pair of 8th notes on beat 1, which are quickly followed on beat 2 by a quarter note. For these passages, feel free to experiment with your right-hand picking. Although the fingerings indicated below the staff suggest using the same finger for all three notes, you can also try alternating your fingers; for example, you could use a middle-ring-middle combo in bar 13, and an index-middle-index combo in bar 15.

STRUM PATTERN:

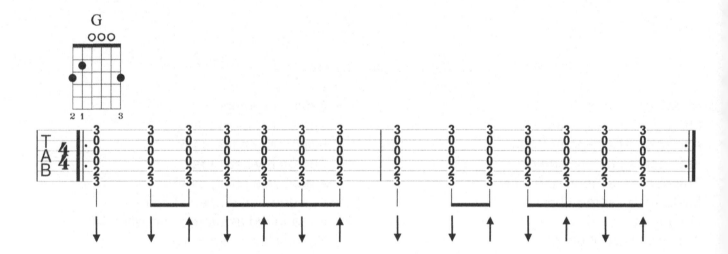

Joy to the World

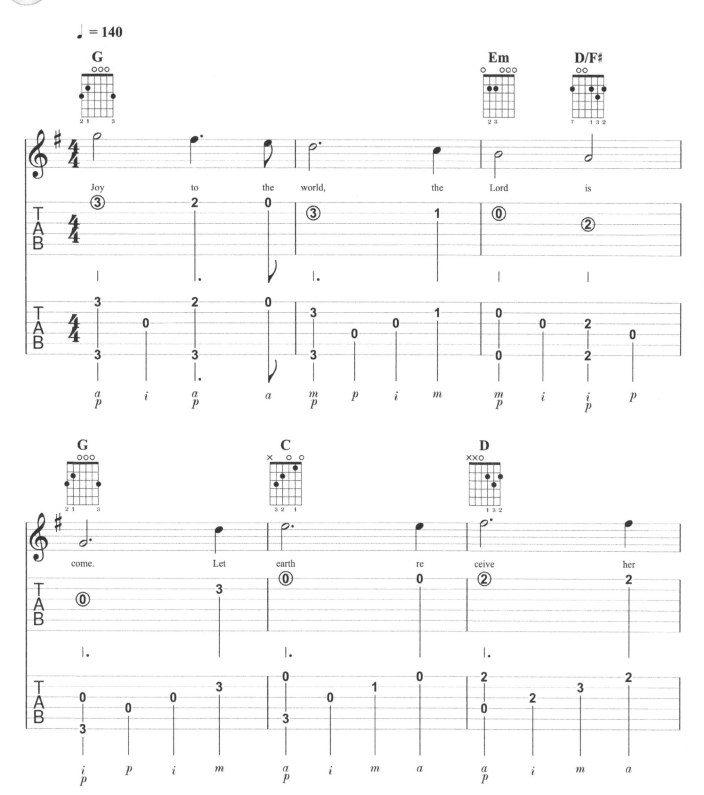

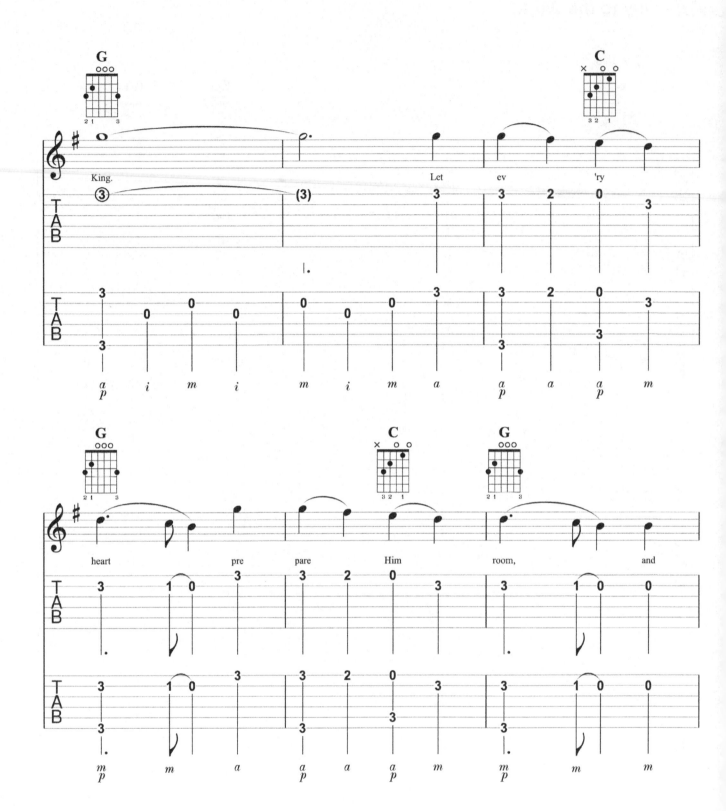

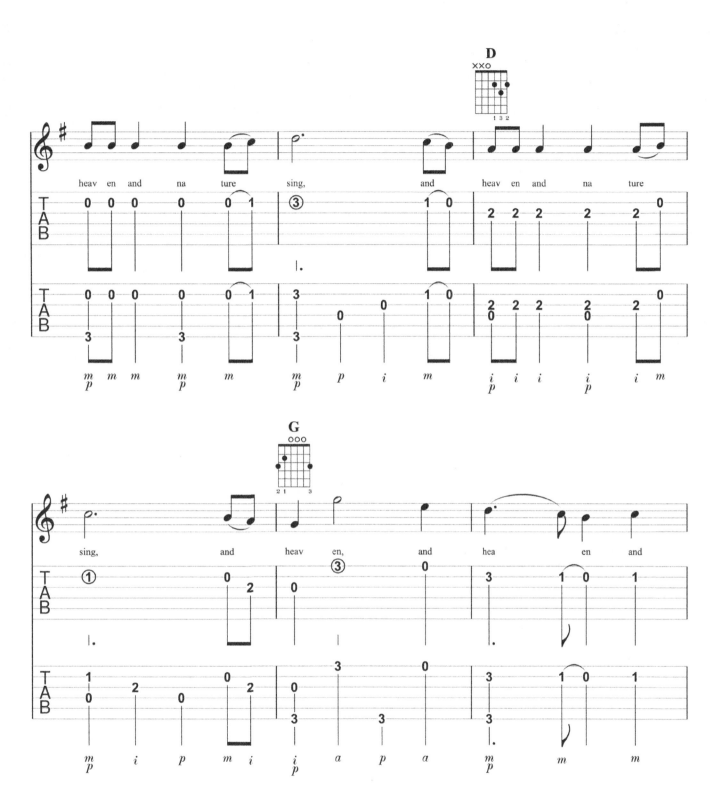

53

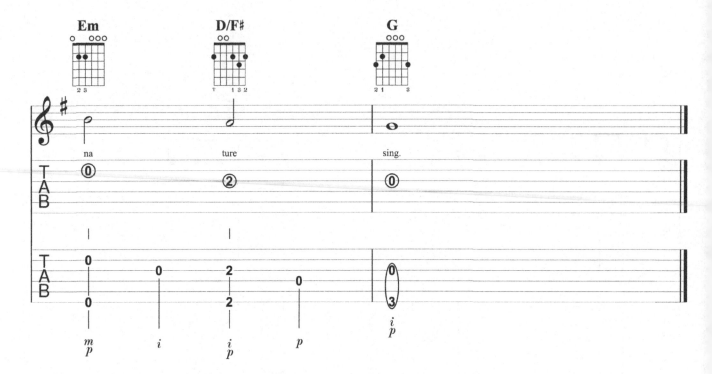

Additional Lyrics

2. Joy to the world, the Savior reigns
   Let men their songs employ
   While fields and floods, rocks, hills, and plains
   Repeat the sounding joy
   Repeat the sounding joy
   Repeat, repeat the sounding joy

3. No more let sins and sorrows grow
   Nor thorns infest the ground
   He comes to make His blessings flow
   Far as the curs is found
   Far as the curse is found
   Far as, far as the curse is found

4. He rules the world with truth and grace
   And makes the nations prove
   The glories of His righteousness
   And wonders of His love
   And wonders of His love
   And wonders, and wonders of His love

O CHRISTMAS TREE

KEY: G

CHORDS: G and D/F♯

TIP: Because of the way the notes change in the melody, you'll need to be strategic with your fret-hand fingerings for the D/F♯ chord change. The best way to perform these passages is with your middle finger on string 6 (fret 2), your ring finger on string 3 (fret 2), and your index finger on string 2 (fret 1). In measures 10–11, where the melody includes the high D note (fret 3, string 2), simply alternate between your index (fret 1) and pinky (fret 3) fingers.

WATCH OUT FOR: The dotted 8th/16th note groupings that open the song (and repeated in bars 5–6 and 13–14). What makes this syncopated rhythm challenging is that it's immediately followed by straight 8th notes. To help you tackle these passages, be sure to listen to the audio tracks to hear how they should sound. Since you're probably familiar with the melody, that works in your favor, as well.

STRUM PATTERN:

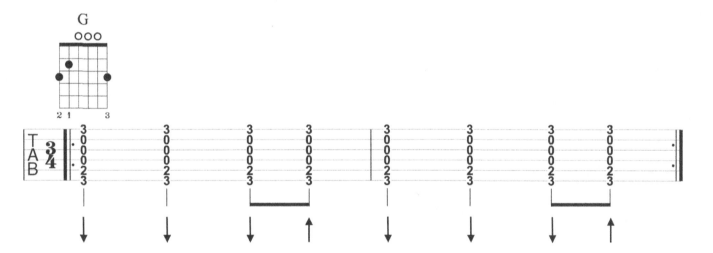

O Christmas Tree

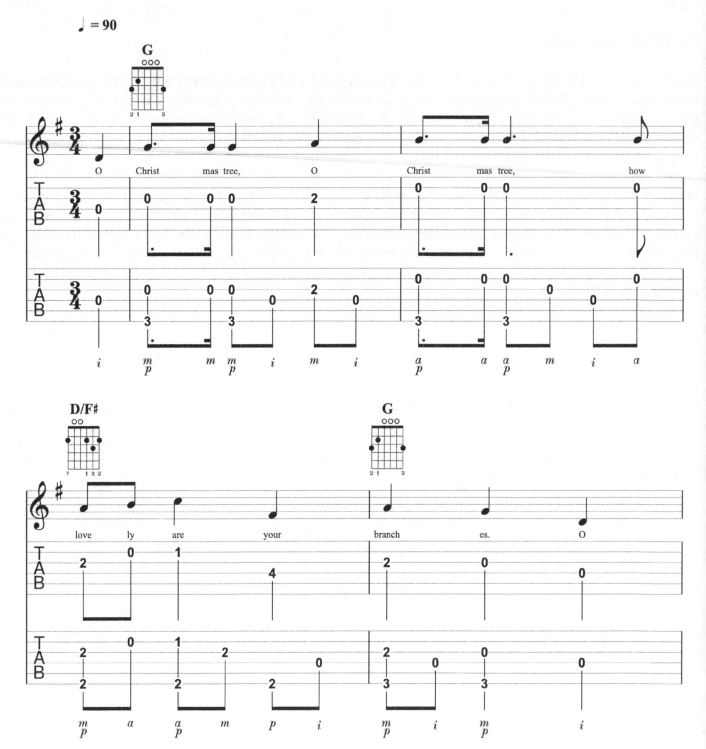

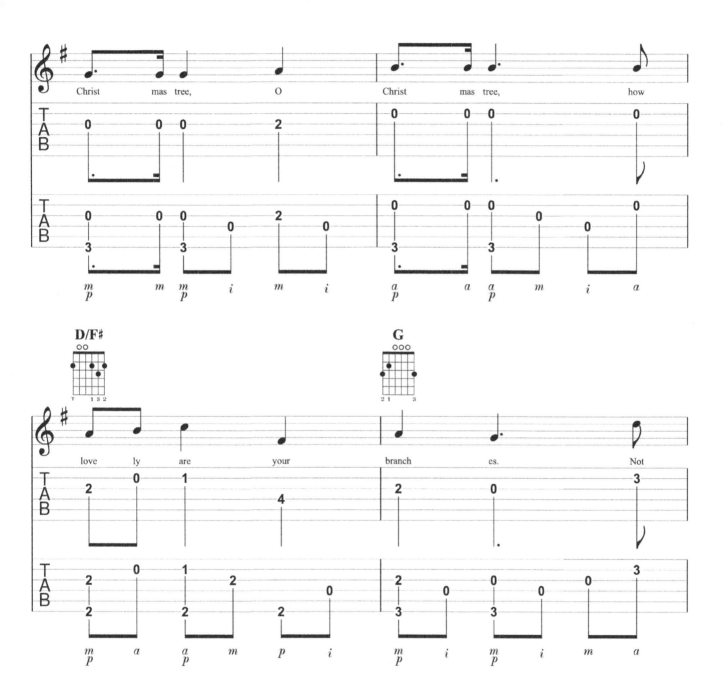

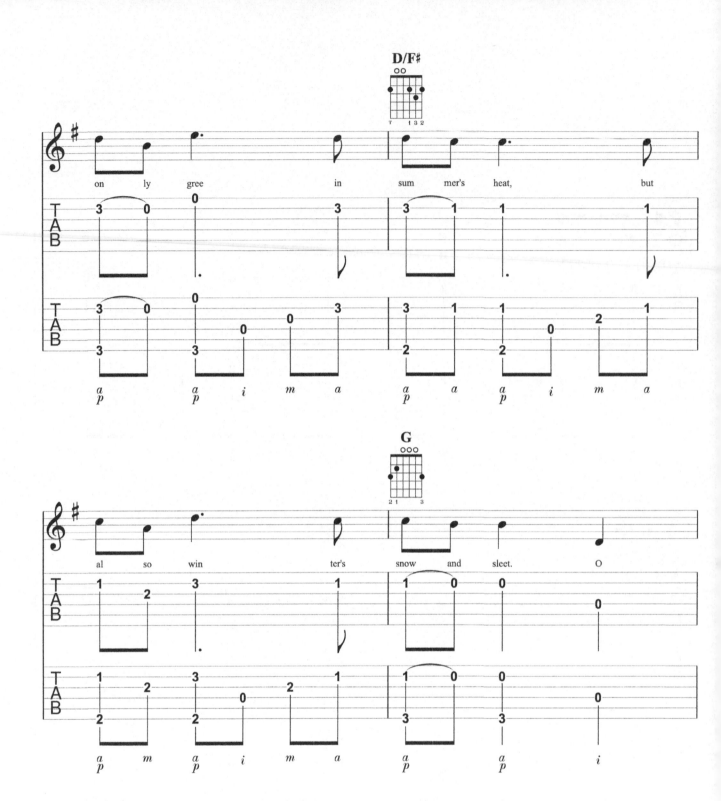

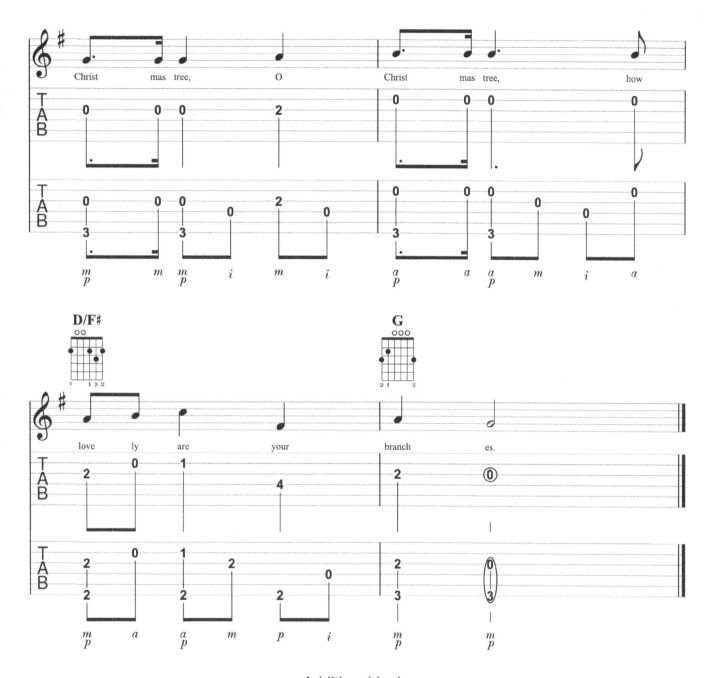

Additional Lyrics

2. O Christmas tree, O Christmas tree,
Of all the trees most lovely
O Christmas tree, O Christmas tree,
Of all the trees most lovely
Each year you bring to us delight
With brightly shining Christmas light
O Christmas tree, O Christmas tree,
Of all the trees most lovely

3. O Christmas tree, O Christmas tree,
We learn from all your beauty
O Christmas tree, O Christmas tree,
We learn from all your beauty
Your bright green leaves with festive cheer
Give hope and strength throughout the year
O Christmas tree, O Christmas tree,
We learn from all your beauty

O COME ALL YE FAITHFUL

KEY: C

CHORDS: C, G, F, Am, Em, and D

TIP: Keep the C chord fretted throughout bars 1–4 of the chorus, using your index and pinky fingers to play the melody notes on strings 1–2. In other words, your ring (fret 3, string 5) and middle (fret 2, string 4) fingers stay affixed to their respective notes/frets while the index and pinky do the heavy lifting.

WATCH OUT FOR: The melody in the 3rd-to-last measure (the G–Am change). On beats 3–4, the melody moves from C (fret 1, string 2) to F (fret 1, string 1), which will require you to roll your index finger from one string to the other. What makes this passage especially challenging is that you'll need to immediately release your index finger to quickly voice the C chord that follows.

STRUM PATTERN:

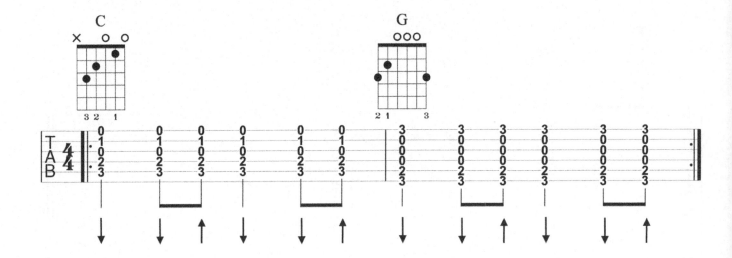

O Come All Ye Faithful

Chorus

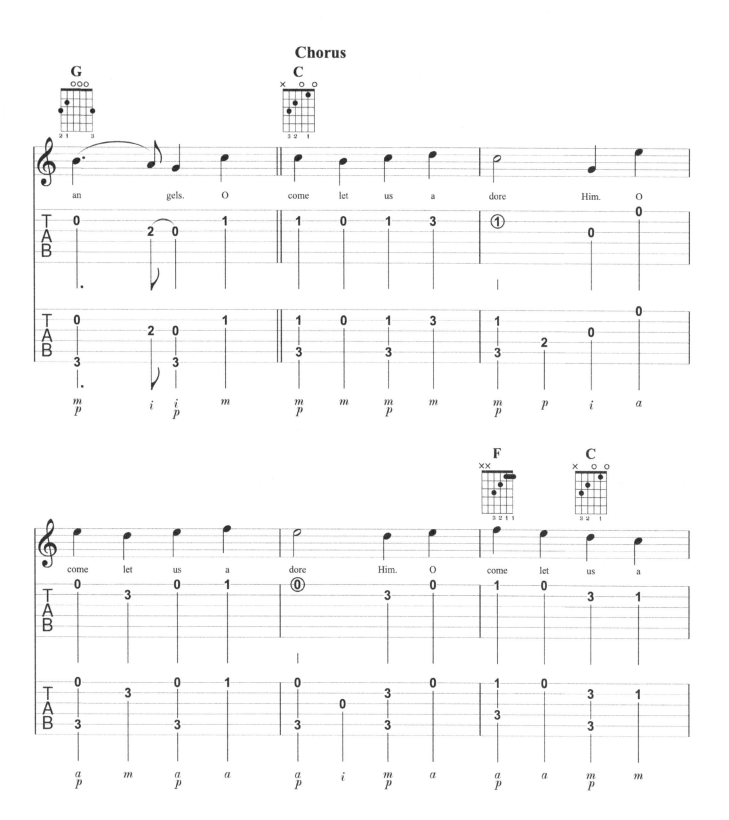

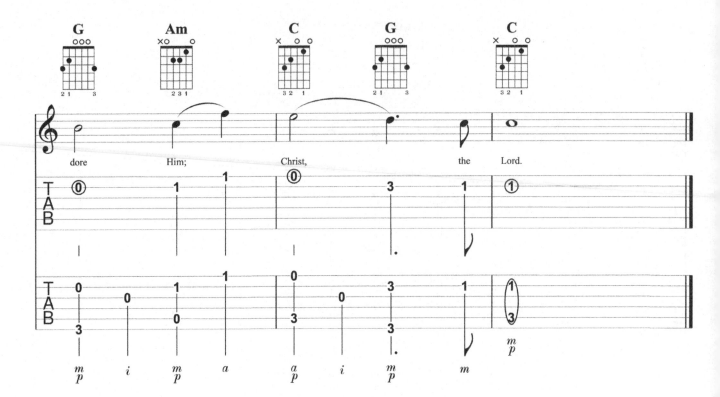

Additional Lyrics

2. Sing, choirs of angels, sing in exultation
   Sing, all ye citizens of heaven above
   Glory to God, Glory in the highest
   O come let us adore him,
   O come let us adore him,
   O come let us adore him;
   Christ, the Lord

3. Yea, Lord, we greet thee, born this happy morning
   Jesus, to thee be all glory given
   Son of the Father, now in flesh appearing
   O come let us adore him,
   O come let us adore him,
   O come let us adore him;
   Christ, the Lord

O COME, O COME EMMANUEL

KEY: Am

CHORDS: Am, Dm, Em, G, and C

TIP: Since only open strings are played in bar 2 of the refrain, you can choose not to voice the Em chord at all; instead, you can use the time to start transitioning your fret hand to the Dm chord that opens bar 3. Although you can't actually fret the Dm chord yet, you *can* begin to form the shape of the chord and quickly clamp down on it when bar 3 arrives.

WATCH OUT FOR: Measure 5 of the verse and measure 6 of the refrain. At first glance, it looks like you just need to voice an open Em chord on beat 3 of these measures. At closer inspection, however, you'll notice that the melody note on fret 2 is actually played on *string 3*, meaning you'll need to incorporate the Esus4 chord that was introduced in the book's introduction. Alternatively, you could simply grab this melody note with your index finger while you pluck string 6 open.

STRUM PATTERN:

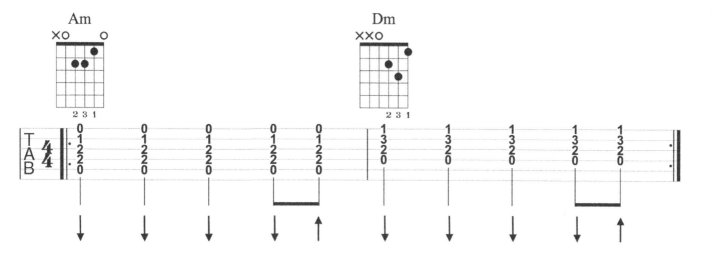

O Come, O Come Emmanuel

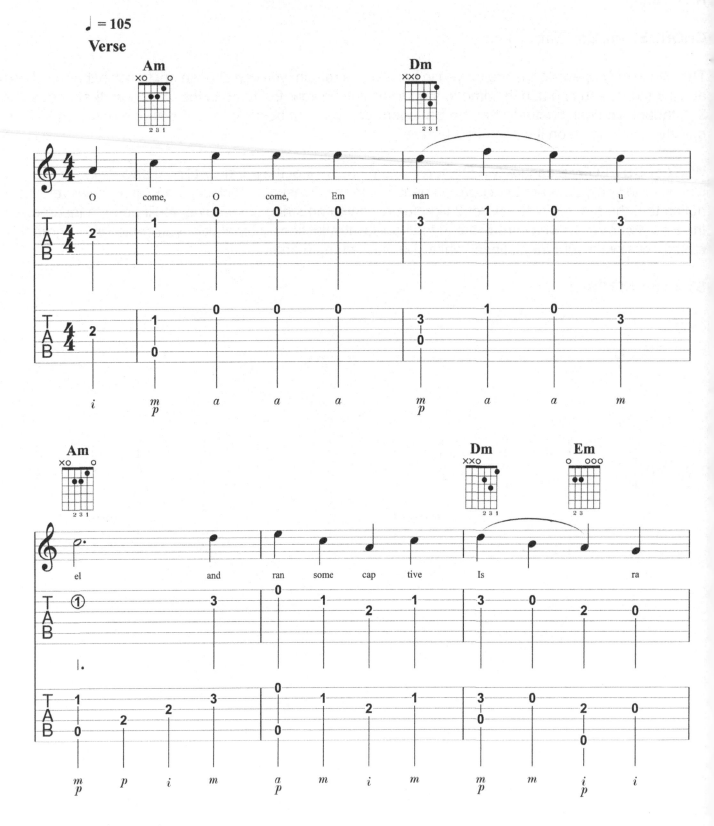

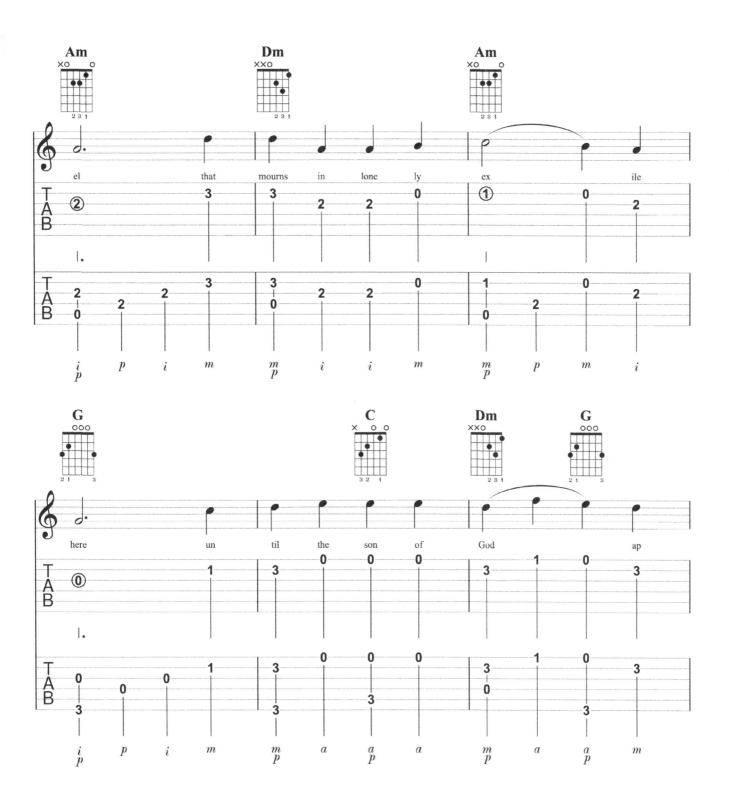

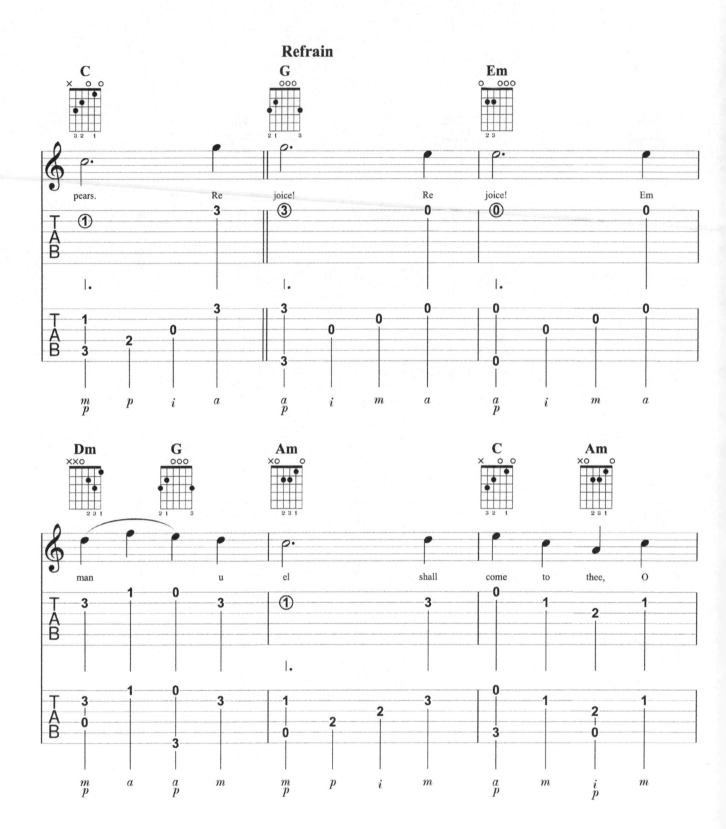

Additional Lyrics

2. O come, Thou Rod of Jesse's tree
   Thine own for Satan's tyranny
   From the depth of hell Thy people save
   And give them victory o'er the grave
   Rejoice! Rejoice! Emmanuel
   Shall come to thee, O Israel

3. O come, Thou Dayspring, from on high
   And cheer us by Thy drawing nigh
   Disperse the gloomy clouds of night
   And death's dark shadows put to flight
   Rejoice! Rejoice! Emmanuel
   Shall come to thee, O Israel

4. O come, Thou Key of David, come
   And open wide our heavenly home
   Make safe the way that leads on high
   And close the path to misery
   Rejoice! Rejoice! Emmanuel
   Shall come to thee, O Israel

5. O come, Adonai, Lord of might
   Who to Thy tribes on Sinai's height
   In ancient times didst give the law
   In cloud and majesty and awe
   Rejoice! Rejoice! Emmanuel
   Shall come to thee, O Israel

O LITTLE TOWN OF BETHLEHEM

KEY: C

CHORDS: C, F, G, A7, Dm, Am, and E

TIP: While the goal in bar 1 (and bar 13) is to allow the low C note (fret 3, string 5) to ring while playing the melody notes on top, this can be quite challenging—if not impossible—while using the standard C chord voicing. To mitigate this problem, feel free to use your middle finger (instead of your ring) to voice this note, which will reduce the amount of stretching needed for your pinky to reach the D♯ note (fret 4, string 2).

WATCH OUT FOR: The slide up to fret 5 in measure 14. The best way to approach this slide is to keep the F chord voiced throughout the measure and add your pinky to fret 3 of string 1 (like you did to begin the measure) on beat 4, and then quickly sliding it up to fret 5. Then, you can simply move the shape back down to fret 3 (and shifting your ring finger from string 4 to string 5) for the C chord that opens measure 15.

STRUM PATTERN:

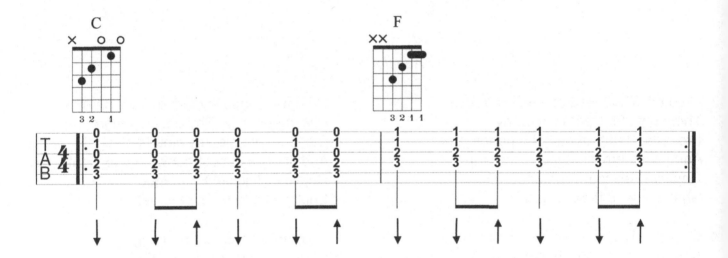

O Little Town of Bethlehem

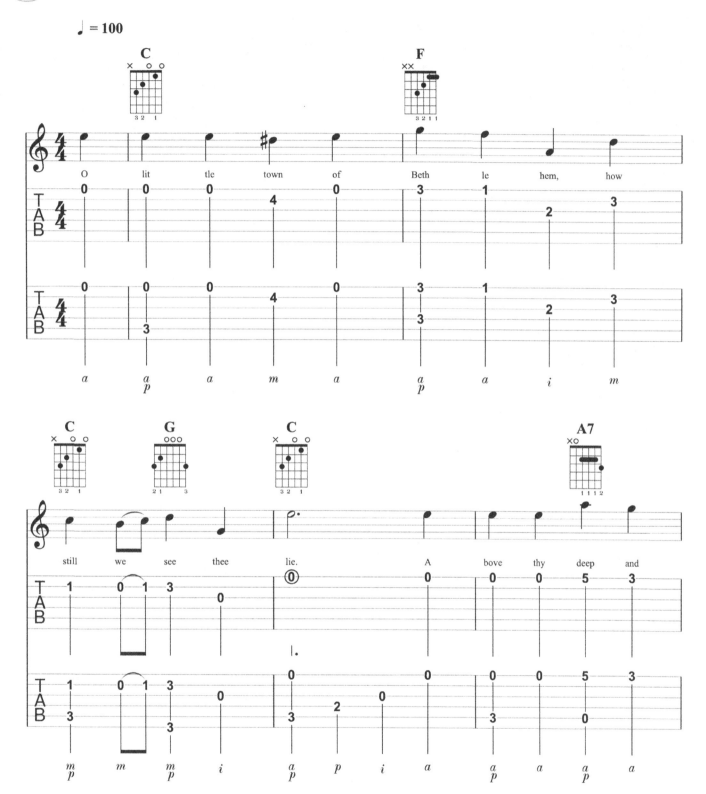

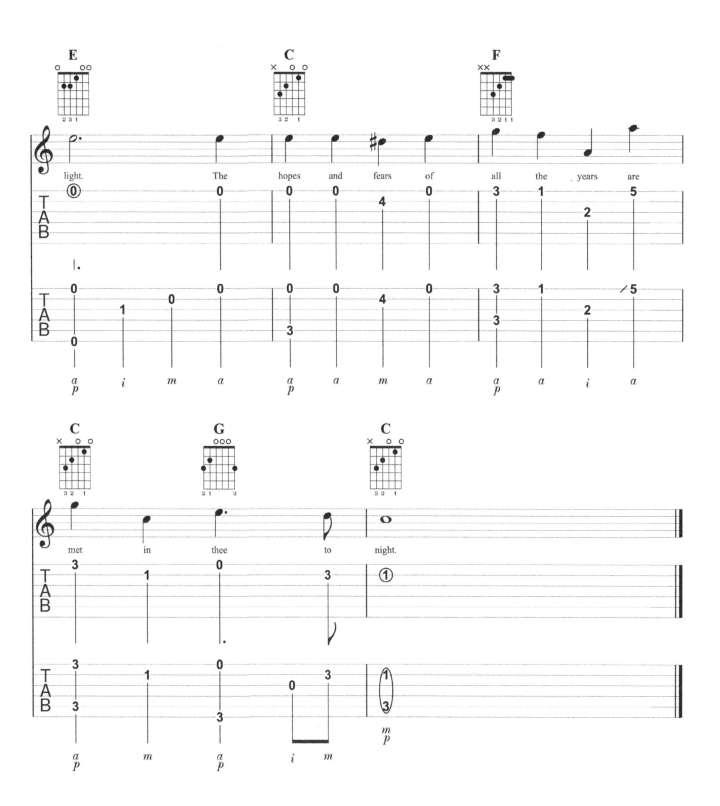

73

Additional Lyrics

2. For Christ is born of Mary
   And gathered all above
   While mortals sleep, the angels keep
   Their watch of wondering love
   O morning stars, together
   Proclaim the holy birth
   And praises sing to God the King
   And peace to all the earth

3. How silently, how silently
   The wonderous gift is given
   So God imparts to human hearts
   The blessings of his heaven
   No ear may hear His coming
   But in this world of sin
   Where meek souls will receive him, still
   The dear Christ enters in

4. O holy Child of Bethlehem
   Descend to us, we pray
   Cast out our sin and enter in
   Be born in us today
   We hear the Christmas angels
   The great, glad tidings tell
   O come to us, abide with us
   Our Lord Emmanuel

SILENT NIGHT

KEY: C

CHORDS: C, G, and F

TIP: In bars 1, 3, 11, and 15, keep your ring finger affixed to fret 3 of string 5 throughout the measure, using the index finger of your fret hand to voice the A note on fret 2 of string 3. This will enable the melody notes to ring out clearly and your middle finger can remain planted on fret 2 of string 4 (for the C chord), as well.

WATCH OUT FOR: The F melody note (fret 3, string 4) in the third-to-last measure. To perform this measure, voice the G chord like the chord frame above the staff suggests; that is, with your middle finger voicing the root note on string 6. That way, you can use your ring finger to grab the F melody note on string 4. This maneuver is more awkward than difficult and shouldn't give you too much trouble. Just be sure to arch your middle finger a little more than usual to give you ring finger enough room to cleanly voice the melody note.

STRUM PATTERN:

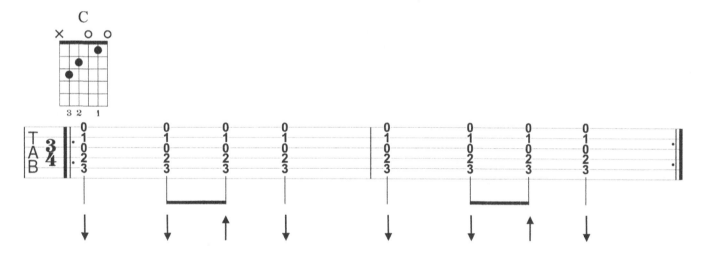

Silent Night

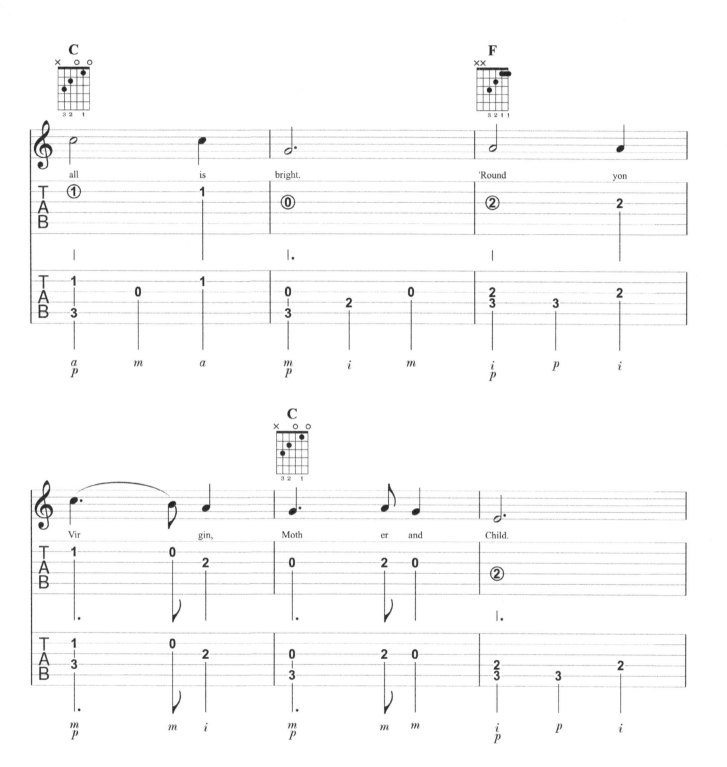

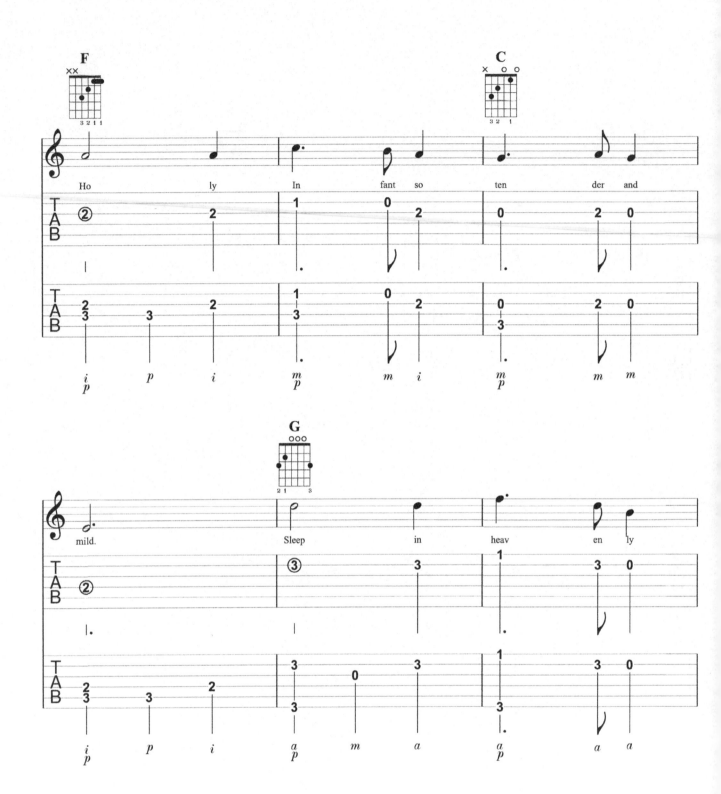

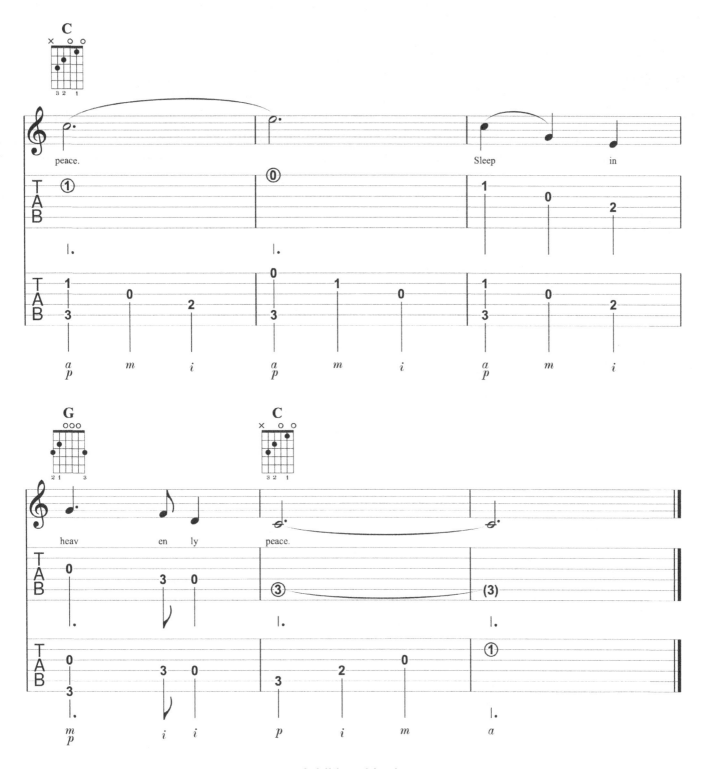

Additional Lyrics

2. Silent night, holy night
   Shepherds quake at the sight
   Glories stream from heaven afar
   Heavenly hosts sing "Alleluia!"
   Christ, the Savior, is born!
   Christ, the Savior, is born!

3. Silent night, holy night
   Son of God, love's pure light
   Radiant beams from Thy holy face
   With the dawn of redeeming grace
   Jesus, Lord, at Thy birth
   Jesus, Lord, at Thy birth

UP ON THE HOUSETOP

KEY: G

CHORDS: G, C, and D

TIP: This song contains several 8th notes and, at the brisk tempo of 130 beats per minute (BPM), can be challenging. The pick-hand fingerings notated below the staff suggest alternating fingers to execute these note groupings, which is the most efficient way to perform the song; however, if you're brand new to fingerstyle guitar, this can be difficult, so a good alternative is to pluck each note of the two-note pairs (on the same string) with the same finger. The downside, of course, is that, the faster the tempo, the more difficult it will be do execute these notes cleanly. Try both methods and use the one that works best for you.

WATCH OUT FOR: The D chord in measure 11. Although the harmony is D major (see the chord frame above the staff), the melody moves to the note C on beat 2, thereby implying a D7 tonality. Therefore, in this measure, you'll want to utilize the D7 chord voicing that was introduced in the book's introduction, rather than the standard open D chord that's used earlier in the song.

STRUM PATTERN:

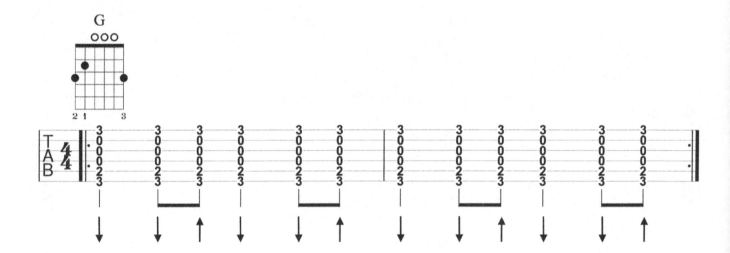

Up on the Housetop

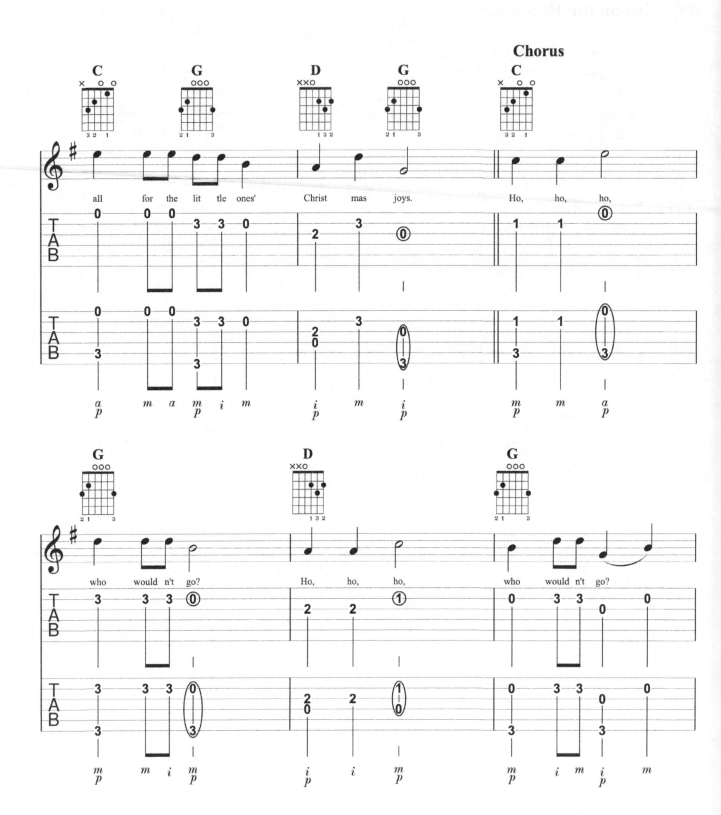

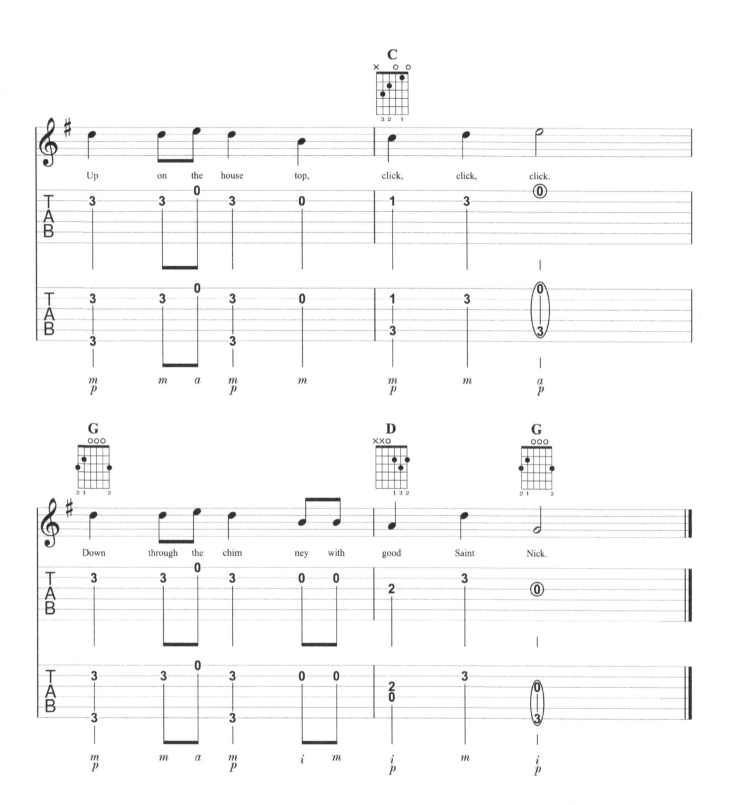

2. First comes the stocking of little Nell
   Oh, dear Santa, fill it well
   Give her a dolly that laughs and cries,
   One that will open and shut her eyes
   Ho, ho, ho, who wouldn't go?
   Ho, ho, ho, who wouldn't go?
   Up on the housetop, click, click, click
   Down through the chimney with good Saint Nick

3. Next comes the stocking of little Will
   Oh, just see what a glorious fill
   Here is a hammer and lots of tacks,
   Also, a ball and a whip that cracks
   Ho, ho, ho, who wouldn't go?
   Ho, ho, ho, who wouldn't go?
   Up on the housetop, click, click, click
   Down through the chimney with good Saint Nick

WE THREE KINGS

KEY: Am

CHORDS: Am, E, G, C, Dm, and F

TIP: Although the song begins with a pair of open strings, you'll want to have your fret hand in place for an open Am chord (see the chord frame above the staff). That way, you can use your pinky to grab the D melody note on beat 3 and your fingers are already in place for the Am chord tones/melody notes that are performed in bar 2.

WATCH OUT FOR: Measure 14. At first glance, it looks like you just need to voice a basic open E chord (the voicing in the frame above the staff). At closer inspection, however, you'll notice that the melody note on fret 1 is actually played on *string 2*, rather than on string 3. Therefore, you really don't need to voice the E chord at all; instead, just voice the note at fret 1 with the index finger of your fret hand while plucking strings 2 and 6 with the thumb and middle finger of your picking hand. Simple.

STRUM PATTERN:

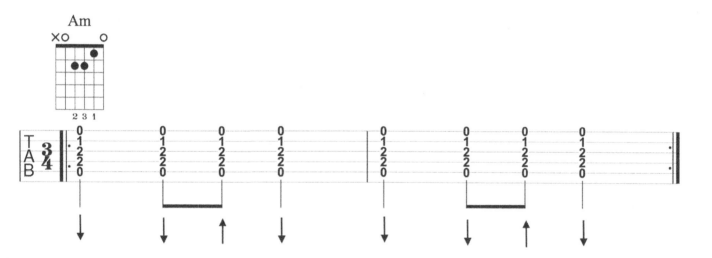

We Three Kings

♩ = 140

Verse

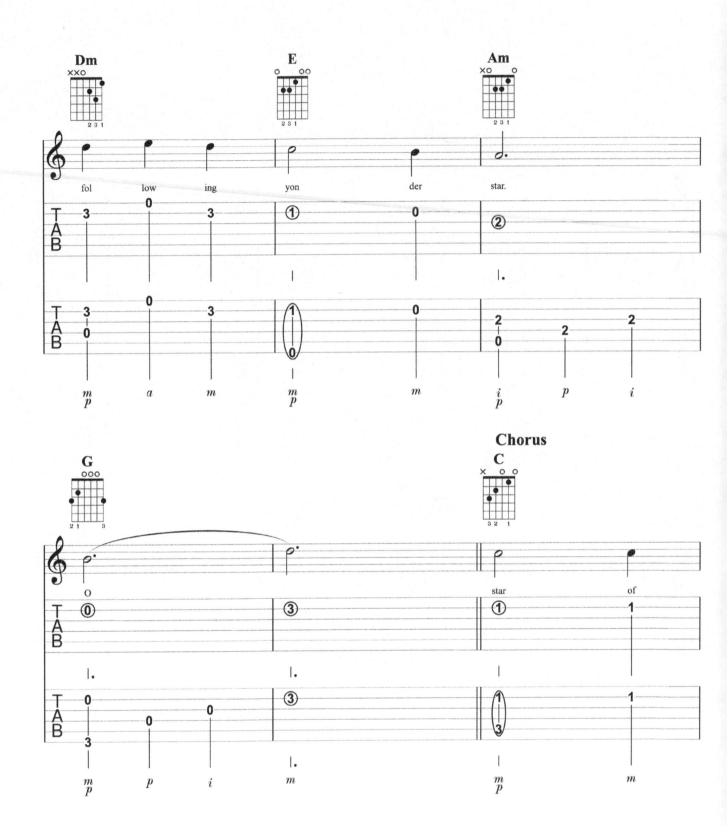

88

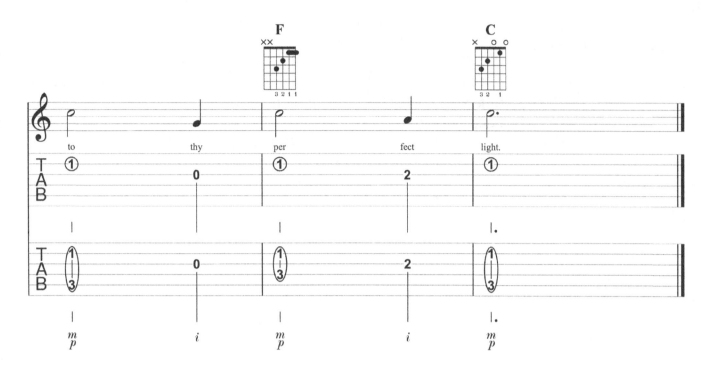

Additional Lyrics

2. Born a King on Bethlehem's plain
   Gold I bring to crown Him again
   King forever, ceasing never
   Over us all to reign
   O star of wonder, star of light
   Star with royal beauty bright
   Westward leading, still proceeding
   Guide us to Thy perfect light

3. Frankincense to offer have I
   Incense owns a Deity nigh
   Prayer and praising, all men raising
   Worship Him, God most high
   O star of wonder, star of light
   Star with royal beauty bright
   Westward leading, still proceeding
   Guide us to Thy perfect light

4. Myrrh is mine, its bitter perfume
   Breathes a life of gathering gloom
   Sorrowing, sighing, bleeding, dying
   Sealed in the stone-cold tomb
   O star of wonder, star of light
   Star with royal beauty bright
   Westward leading, still proceeding
   Guide us to Thy perfect light

5. Glorious now, behold Him arise
   King and God and sacrifice
   Alleluia, Alleluia
   Earth to heaven replies
   O star of wonder, star of light
   Star with royal beauty bright
   Westward leading, still proceeding
   Guide us to Thy perfect light

WE WISH YOU A MERRY CHRISTMAS

KEY: C

CHORDS: C, F, D, and G

TIP: This song contains a lot of fast-moving (8th-note) melody notes that are difficult to pluck at 120 beats per minute (BPM). Therefore, hammer-on and pull-off articulations are included throughout the arrangement. If these techniques are new to you, they basically involve picking just the first note of each two-note pair and then "hammering" onto or "pulling" off from the string. In other words, you pluck the first note normally, but then sound the second note via the actions of your fret hand—hence the terms "pull-off" and "hammer-on."

WATCH OUT FOR: Measure 3. Start this measure by voicing a standard open D chord (see the chord frame above the staff) but leaving the top string open. On beat 3, you'll need to simultaneously pull off from fret 3 with your ring finger (which is already in place because of the D chord) while reaching down with your index finger to grab fret 1. Fortunately, the note just prior to the pull-off is an open string, which gives you a head start on transitioning your index finger to fret 1.

STRUM PATTERN:

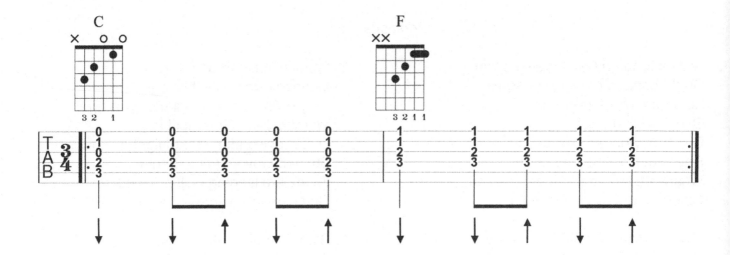

We Wish You a Merry Christmas

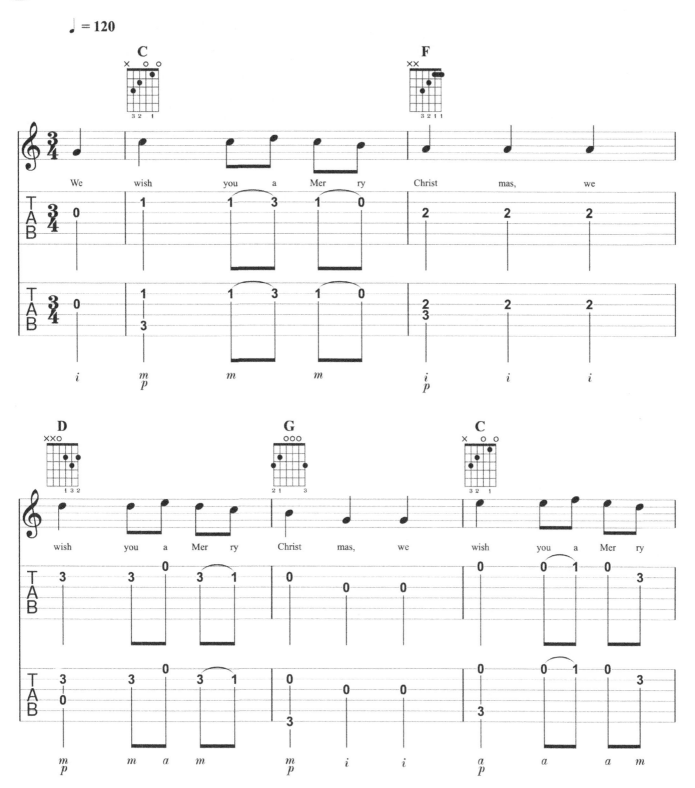

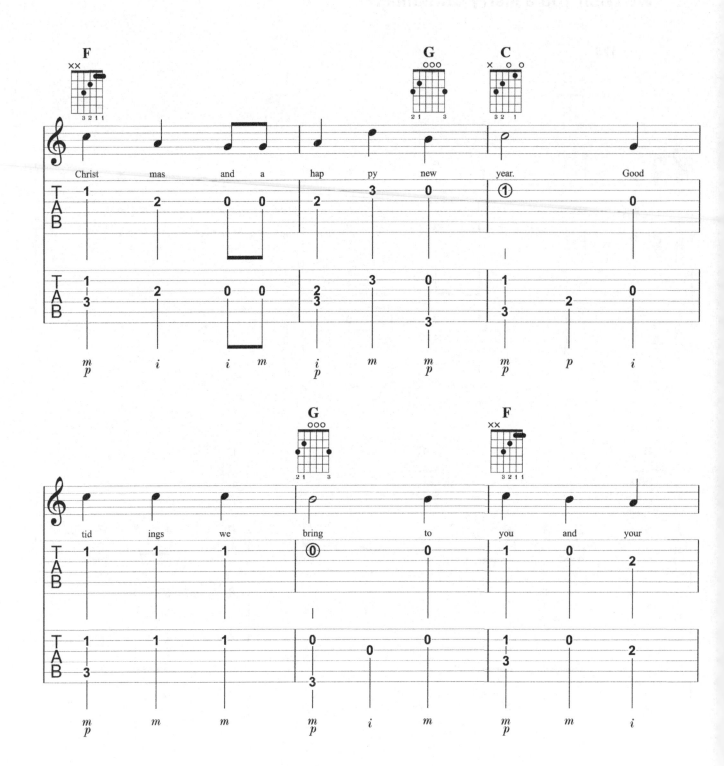

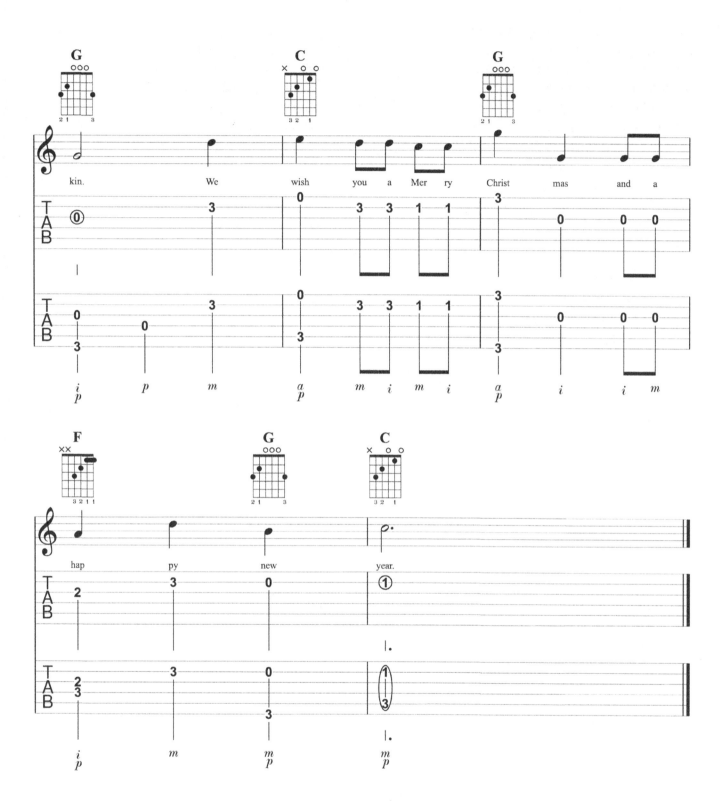

Additional Lyrics

2. Oh, bring us some figgy pudding
   Oh, bring us some figgy pudding
   Oh, bring us some figgy pudding
   And bring it right here
   Good tidings we bring
   To you and your kin
   We wish you a Merry Christmas
   And a happy new year

4. We all like our figgy pudding
   We all like our figgy pudding
   We all like our figgy pudding
   With all its good cheer
   Good tidings we bring
   To you and your kin
   We wish you a Merry Christmas
   And a happy new year

3. We won't go until we get some
   We won't go until we get some
   We won't go until we get some
   So, bring it right here
   Good tidings we bring
   To you and your kin
   We wish you a Merry Christmas
   And a happy new year

5. We wish you a Merry Christmas
   We wish you a Merry Christmas
   We wish you a Merry Christmas
   And a happy new year

Made in the USA
Las Vegas, NV
27 November 2023

81610824R00057